Apostles, Apostolic People and Churches

*Understanding God's Blueprint
for Leadership in the 21st Century*

Robert Munien

Apostles, Apostolic People and Churches
by Robert Munien

Copyright © 1999 — Robert Munien

ISBN 1-58169-027-4
For Worldwide Distribution
Printed in the U.S.A.

Gazelle Press
An Imprint of Genesis Communications, Inc.
P.O. Box 91011 • Mobile, AL 36691
(334) 665-0022 • 888-670-7463
Email: GenesisCom@aol.com

Dedication

This book is dedicated to the Apostle and High Priest of our confession Jesus Christ, Hebrews 3:1, whose grace and faithfulness has enabled the completion of this book.

To my love, companion and closest friend, Judy. My children Candice and Emile' who have taught me to love and be loved. My gratitude goes beyond these printed words.

Acknowledgments

I must thank all those whom the Lord has used in my life: Dr. Noel Woodroffe—my covenant friend whose life has challenged and encouraged me. The WBN family, the AFM and the great leaders who have impacted my life over the years. To Pastor Jerome and Becky Johns, Mark and Debbie Holcomb, Dr. S.Y. Govender, Pastor Joe D' Allende and Pastor Victor David, who have inspired me to be all that the Lord wants me to be. To my mum and family who have prayed and supported our ministry over the years—thank you.

My gratitude to my efficient secretary, Gilinda Gopal, who typed the manuscripts; team members, Leon and Heather Naidoo, Jafeth and Charmayne Brijmohan; Vishal Jets and Selvan and Vernie Padayachee—thank you guys for your belief and support to me over the years.

My very special thanks to Eugene and Karen Strite, my covenant friends who have been a source of blessing and strength. Your love, care and moral and financial support has made this project possible.

My thanks to my friend Larry Walker and his company for their gracious work with this manuscript.

Contents

Foreword

It is undeniable that the greatest move of God since Pentecost is now taking place in the global Church. The Spirit of the Lord is preparing us for the push toward ultimate fulfillment of all the purposes of the Lord. In this present time, the Lord has released and restored the ministry gift of the apostle to the Church. For the first time since the days of the Book of the Acts of the Apostles, the general Church is recognizing, understanding, receiving and honoring the governmental ministry gift of the apostle and the other four governmental ascension gifts of prophet, evangelist, pastor and teacher. This is a time of unprecedented favor and unmatched potential and strength in the people of God.

No longer is the Church operating in an escapist mentality and hiding out behind walls of provincialism and limitation. It has emerged into the majestic world of global strategic action and accurate advances in the purposes of the Lord. The spiritual ears of the people of God have been tuned to the cutting edge frequencies of the authoritative positions of the third millennium and the government of the Kingdom of God is being manifested in all quarters of the global Church.

This transformation, restructuring and Reformation of the Church is being directed and led by the apostles of the Church raised up in this hour in every society and in every spiritual jurisdiction of the earth. No longer is the word of the Lord confined and recognized in only one quarter of the Church. In every corner of the planet the commanding utterances of the apostles are stirring the Church from lethargy and spiritual torpor into excellence, accuracy and powerful spiritual action. We are on the move at last and will not stop until His final work is done!

The LORD of hosts has sworn, saying, "Surely, as I have thought, so it shall come to pass, and as I have purposed, so it shall stand: That I will break the Assyrian in My land, and on My mountains tread him underfoot. Then his yoke shall be removed from them, and his burden removed from their shoulders. This is the purpose that is purposed against the whole earth, and this is the hand that is stretched out over all the nations. For the LORD of hosts has purposed, and who will annul it? His hand is stretched out, and who will turn it back?" (Is. 14:24-27)

Robert Munien is an apostle from South Africa and has emerged out of the prophetic release of that nation from apartheid and psychological servitude to bring to us a clear word of instruction and impartation concerning apostles, apostolic churches and apostolic people. His book is not an inaccessible document, but a clear statement designed to equip the saints. It brings the Church to a place of operational competence in its understanding of this important ministry gift, and the nature of its operation in building the individual and corporate lives of the people of God. It is a timely volume and is a must-read for all Kingdom people wishing to inform themselves of the current developments in the Church today. I urge you to read and study this book carefully and to receive the apostolic impartation that it carries.

Robert, as a member of the apostolic team of the World Breakthrough Network, represents not only his local church in Durban, South Africa, his nation and his continent of Africa, but also the associated churches, ministries and Kingdom organizations of his Network spread across more than thirty nations of the earth.

I highly commend both Apostle Robert Munien and this book to you.

Dr. Noel Woodroffe
Founder and Leader of the Apostolic Team
World Breakthrough Network
Apostle@wbnetwork.org

Introduction

As we prepare to enter a new millennium or new day in God, there are paradigm shifts that are taking place all over the world. Economies and nations around the world are being pressured into change. The spirit of reformation has entered into life of the global Church. Set ideologies and mentalities that have entrapped and conditioned our behaviour, are being challenged. God is demanding transformation and is reconfiguring the operating system of the global Church. The global Church is in a state of transition. The Spirit of the Lord is summoning us to accurately define our position, thinking patterns and attitudes.

The present generation of apostolic leadership has been chosen by our Lord Jesus Christ to usher in an awakening of the apostolic ministry that over the centuries had been neglected. No doubt there have been sprinklings throughout the Church Age, but never as dynamic as now. God is accelerating the culmination of His eternal will upon the Global

Church. God had promised that the latter house shall be greater than the former house (Haggai 2:9). The restoration of the Apostolic and Prophetic ministries is God's ordained means of unveiling God's purposes for the Twenty First Century. Like Jeremiah these present day servants of the Lord are appointed and anointed over the nations over the kingdoms, to root out, pull down, and to destroy, and to throw down, to build and to plant (Jer. 1:10).

My deepest desire is that this book will bring a clear understanding upon the global Church of present day Apostles, their ministries and impartations, strategy to transition the church into an apostolic paradigm that an apostolic people be birthed.

Chapter 1

The Gift of an Apostle

*Now therefore ye are no more strangers and foreigners, but fellowcitizens with the saints, and of the household of God; and **are built upon the foundation of the apostles** and prophets, Jesus Christ himself being the chief corner stone* (Ephesians 2:19-20).

There is a story that has been around for generations, and it has as many variations as it has years of existence. Nevertheless, let me share the version I remember:

A man working in a ditch was asked what he was doing and he replied, "I'm digging a hole for something. Ask that man over there if you need to know more." When the other man, who appeared to be working with stone was asked the same question, he said, "I'm laying block for the foundation of a building." Another man stood on a small rise surveying the entire expanse of the project. When he was asked what he was doing, he said, "Why, I'm building the Cathedral of Notre Dame, my young man."

When God launches a grand building project of eternal magnitude, He carefully calls and equips people of many different talents and gifts.

Most are faithful laborers who work hard and supply vital labor in virtually every area of the Church. Others are born builders who build line by line and precept upon precept according to the design given to them. Some specialize on walls, others on support beams, and still others on the high flying buttresses that require specialized gifts and equipment.

Rarest of all are the men like the one interviewed last in my story—the architects and overseers of the major components of the project. These are no more special than anyone else, except that it is their task to see the big picture at all times and to faithfully shape, prepare, and direct the wise placement of materials, gifts, and workers in the right place at the right time. They also bear the weight and risk of failure and faith at all times. These are the apostles of the Church of Jesus Christ.

Paul said Jesus Christ gave five "equipping" or "ascension" gifts to the Church: apostles, prophets, evangelists, pastors, and teachers (see Eph. 4:8-13). Of the five ascension gifts, two are called foundational gifts by Paul in Ephesians 2:20. His words are just as crucial to the Church today as they were in his day. The earthly household of God is "...built on the foundation of the apostles and prophets" (Eph. 2:20a).

Nearly every major church body in organized Christianity will agree that the messianic prophecies of the Old Testament and the foundational teachings and church-planting work of the first apostles in the first century are valid and vital works of God wrought through mortal men. The agreement begins

2

to disintegrate from this point on, despite the words of Paul in his letter to the Ephesians:

Wherefore he saith, When he ascended up on high, he led captivity captive, and gave gifts unto men. (Now that he ascended, what is it but that he also descended first into the lower parts of the earth? He that descended is the same also that ascended up far above all heavens, that he might fill all things.) ***And he gave some, apostles; and some, prophets; and some, evangelists; and some, pastors and teachers;*** *for the **perfecting of the saints,** for the **work of the ministry,** for the **edifying of the body** of Christ* (Ephesians 4:8-12).

We know that the Church began under the inspired ministry and leadership of the apostles and continued to expand among the Gentile nations in the same way. But I propose that the Holy Spirit has once again been preparing apostles in the midst of the Church. This cadre of anointed leaders has been hidden and unrecognized, and many of them have at times also questioned whether the ministry office and the function of apostles still exist in the Church today.

The truth is that apostles have always been in the Church throughout history, although they have not always been recognized and received as apostles. Ironically, many of the people whom God has used as apostles in recent years were themselves actively preaching that apostles ceased to exist after the original apostles died in the first century!

The Holy Spirit has used the gifts and ministry of apostles to birth movements in every new season in the Church. The same Lord who declared, "I will build my church" (Matt. 16:18b) is openly restoring the office of the apostle to the Church just as He restored the office of the prophet in recent years. I say "restored" because the clearly supernatural gifts of apostle and prophet were laid aside and dismissed in the same era of error that "lost" the truths of salvation by faith and the priesthood of all believers!

Just as He "restored" the unchanging truths of salvation by faith, the power of the blood, the priesthood of believers, and the continued existence and importance of the baptism of the Holy Spirit and the nine grace or *"charis"* gifts, He is re-emphasizing the need and importance of the apostolic gift in the Church today. It is no accident or coincidence that as we enter the twenty-first century, God is giving prominence to a worldwide apostolic movement that is unequaled in modern Church history.

Jesus Embodied All Five Leadership Gifts

God's Word boldly declares, "For in him [Jesus Christ] dwelleth all the fulness of the Godhead bodily" (Col. 2:9).

All that God is, was contained and embodied in Jesus Christ. And Paul tells us that Jesus imparted to the many-membered Church all that the Father gave Him! (See John 17:14-24.) Among the many gifts the Lord placed in the Church were the ascension or equipping gifts of apostle, prophet, evangelist, teacher, and pastor (see Eph. 4:11-13).

It is in these gifts that we find the mantle and anointing Jesus demonstrated in His earthly ministry in the first century. These gifts are given to mature, edify, activate, and equip the saints for ministry.

1. *Pastor.* "I am the good shepherd; the good shepherd giveth his life for the sheep" (John 10:11).
2. *Teacher.* "And he opened his mouth, and taught them..." (Matt. 5:2).
3. *Evangelist.* "For the Son of man is come to save that which was lost" (Matt. 18:11). "The Spirit of the Lord is upon me, because he hath anointed me

to preach the gospel to the poor; he hath sent me to heal the brokenhearted, to preach deliverance to the captives, and recovering of sight to the blind, to set at liberty them that are bruised" (Luke 4:18; see also 15:3-7).

4. *Prophet.* "And they were offended in him. But Jesus said unto them, A prophet is not without honour, save in his own country, and in his own house" (Matt. 13:57).

5. *Apostle.* "Wherefore, holy brethren, partakers of the heavenly calling, consider the Apostle and High Priest of our profession, Christ Jesus" (Heb. 3:1).

God did *not* give these ascension or leadership gifts to the Church so He could recreate the priestly hierarchy and sacrificial system that He sent Jesus to dismantle through the shedding of His own blood. Nor did He wish to recreate a system of earthly "mediators" between God and man. He declares in His Word, "For there is one God, and *one mediator* between God and men, the man Christ Jesus" (1 Tim. 2:5).

These gifts are anointings given bodily to the Church for the primary purpose of equipping the saints "for the work of the ministry" (Eph. 4:11).

What Does "Apostle" Mean?

The word *apostle* is a "transliterated" word that was carried over and incorporated in the English language exactly as it sounds in the Greek. It literally means "messenger" or "he that is sent."[1]

According to *Thayer's Greek Lexicon*, the Greek word transliterated as "apostle" refers to "a delegate messenger, one sent forth with orders. Apostle has a simple meaning from classical Greek literature: one sent as a representative of another. The representative deriving his authority and power from the one who is sending him."[2] The one sent serves as an ambassador, or a representative of highest rank sent to a foreign country.

Kevin Conner differentiated between the classical and *koine* or common Greek usages of *apostolos*, or apostle:

"The classical Greek has various usages:
1. A naval expedition, a cargo ship, a fleet of ships sent with a specific objective.
2. The admiral or commander of the naval expedition or fleet of ships.
3. The colony which was founded by the admiral, a group of colonists sent overseas.
4. A personal convoy or emissary or ambassador, a delegate. The usage connects the SENDER AND THE SENT ONE."[3]

Conner writes in his book, *Church in the New Testament*, that the *koine* or common street Greek use of *apostolos* referred to "a commissioned messenger or ambassador, delegate, one who is sent forth, one commissioned and authorized by another to represent another and carry out his will and purposes. The sent one is one with the one who sent him."[4]

It is reasonable for us to conclude that an apostle—even in our day—is a "sent one," an ambassador who is connected to the sender. One of the greatest sources of confusion about apostles comes from a poor understanding of the types of apostles appearing in the New Testament record and how they compare to apostles today.

The Apostle of the Father

Jesus referred to Himself as "one sent by the Father," which made Him the one and only "apostle of the Father," the personal envoy and ambassador of the Ancient of Days. Jesus is the First and Senior Apostle (the Lord of lords and King of kings), sent on a mission to redeem mankind for God the Father. This is specifically referred to in the Book of Hebrews: "Wherefore, holy brethren, partakers of the heavenly calling, consider the Apostle and High Priest of our profession, Christ Jesus" (Heb. 3:1).

Apostles of the Lamb

Then said Jesus to them again, Peace be unto you: as my Father hath sent me, even so send I you (John 20:21).

After His resurrection from the dead, Jesus appeared to the apostles and commissioned the eleven to continue what He had begun. The Twelve (Matthias was added to take the place of Judas Iscariot) are called "the apostles of the Lamb," and they have a special place of honor in the Church.

They were the original "sent ones"; they were personally commissioned by the Messiah to be living witnesses to the sinless life, miraculous ministry, sacrificial death, and supernatural resurrection of the Lamb.

It was the Twelve who were anointed to preach the good news (the gospel) and to anchor and nurture the infant Church "born in a day." It was the eyewitness testimony of the Twelve that served as the basis for the four Gospel accounts. It was their task to set forth the unchanging foundation of the Risen Christ and Messiah for the generations to follow.

The Apostle by Revelation

One more apostle was called and commissioned personally by the risen Christ—Saul of Tarsus, who was later known as the apostle Paul.

In the eyes of Paul, of the community of Pharisees in Jerusalem, and of the persecuted Christian community, there was no more unlikely candidate for apostleship than Saul the zealous persecutor and hunter of Christians. Yet God saw things differently. Jesus arrested Saul on the Damascus road and changed his direction forever. (See Acts 9:3-6.) In the end, almost 75 percent of our New Testament Scriptures were penned by Paul, the "chiefest of sinners" (see 1 Tim. 1:15).

Apostles of the Holy Spirit

So they, being sent forth by the Holy Ghost, departed unto Seleucia; and from thence they sailed to Cyprus (Acts 13:4).

Apostles are a prominent part of Christ's "ascension gifts" to the Church. They are the gifts of a Bridegroom to His Bride to prepare and equip her for the great wedding feast of the Lamb. Until that great feast, apostles will always function in the Church, equipping and ministering to Christ's Body in the earth along with prophets, evangelists, pastors, and teachers.

There are four key terms used in the New Testament to describe the function and role of apostles in the plans and purposes of God for the Church: first, wise master builders, pioneers, and "commissioned ones."

First Apostles

*And God hath set some in the church, **first apostles**, secondarily prophets, thirdly teachers, after that miracles, then gifts of healings, helps, governments, diversities of tongues* (1 Corinthians 12:28).

The Greek word translated as "first" in this verse is *proton*. According to James Strong, it means "first, firstly in time, place, order or importance; before, at the beginning, first of all, chiefly, of rank or dignity; first in rank, influence, honor, chief principal."[5]

The office of the apostle was the first ministry Jesus established at the beginning of the Church Age. Although the office was gradually lost or dismissed as invalid in the Dark Ages, the work of apostles still continued under other titles or descriptions. The apostolic ministry also will be the last ministry restored and established in this worldwide apostolic movement.

Apostles supernaturally impart into the life of the saints the anointing of the "sent ones." Saints who possess the anointing and calling of "sent ones" instinctively set out to finish the work of world evangelism and church planting, primarily by establishing new works and by raising up and setting into place other members of the five ascension equipping ministries to equip the Body of Christ.

The Wise Master Builders of the Kingdom

According to the grace of God which is given unto me, ***as a wise masterbuilder, I have laid the foundation****, and another buildeth thereon. But let every man take heed how he buildeth thereupon* (1 Corinthians 3:10).

The Greek word translated as "wise masterbuilder" in this verse is *architekton*. It means "chief constructor, i.e., architect, master builder."[6] *Architekton* is the root word from which we get the English word *architect*. According to *Webster's Ninth New Collegiate Dictionary*, an architect is "one who designs buildings and advises in their construction, and one who plans and achieves a difficult objective."[7]

Apostles build according to design, pattern, or blueprint, even though they are considered the "architects" among the five equipping and leadership gifts. That is because apostles are also "under authority," and they follow the plan of God, not their own. When God asked Moses to build a tabernacle, He gave him the pattern on the mountain. Long before that time, when God told Noah to build an ark, he built it according to the pattern of God.

Make yourself an ark of gopherwood; make rooms in the ark, and cover it inside and outside with pitch (Genesis 6:14 NKJV).

Then Moses went up, also Aaron, Nadab, and Abihu, and seventy of the elders of Israel (Exodus 24:9 NKJV).

Then David gave his son Solomon the plans for the portico of the temple, its buildings, its storerooms, its upper parts, its inner rooms and the place of atonement (1 Chronicles 28:11 NIV).

See that you make all things according to the pattern shown you on the mountain (Hebrews 8:5c NKJV).

Endnotes

1. James Strong, *Strong's Exhaustive Concordance of the Bible* (Peabody, MA: Hendrickson Publishers, n.d.), **apostle** (Greek, #652).
2. Carl L.W. Grimm, *A Greek-English Lexicon of the New Testament*, trans., rev., and enl. by Joseph Henry Thayer (Grand Rapids, MI: Baker Book House, 1970, 1977).
3. Kevin J. Conner, *Church in the New Testament* (Chichester, England: Sovereign World, 1980).
4. Conner, *Church in the New Testament*.
5. Strong's, **first** (Greek, #4412).
6. Strong's, **wise masterbuilder** (Greek, #753).
7. *Webster's Ninth New Collegiate Dictionary* (Springfield, MA: Merriam-Webster Inc., Publishers, 1991), 101.

Chapter 2

Apostles: Moving the Stones Into Position

Whenever God gave men the task of building something for Him, He always gave them the pattern, design, and blueprint by which they were to build and construct His desire. Apostles are God's master builders, leaders who are gifted with wisdom and insight by the Spirit to direct construction, which includes the equipping and placement of the lively stones of God into precise position in His temple.

There is a strong Old Testament precedent for the careful placement of "stones" that carries over into the New Covenant of grace. When Solomon built the temple of God, he gave specific instructions (passed down from his father David) about the shaping (equipping and preparation) of the stones and how they were to be set in place at the temple site.

And the king commanded, and they brought great stones, costly stones, and hewed stones, to lay the foundation

*of the house. And Solomon's builders and Hiram's
builders did hew them, and the stonesquarers: so they
prepared timber and stones to build the house* (1 Kings
5:17-18).

*And the house, when it was in building, was built of
stone **made ready before it was brought thither:** so
that there was neither hammer nor axe nor any tool of
iron heard in the house, while it was in building*
(1 Kings 6:7).

*Ye also, as lively stones, are built up a spiritual house,
an holy priesthood, to offer up spiritual sacrifices,
acceptable to God by Jesus Christ* (1 Peter 2:5).

The stones that were used to build the Temple of Solomon
and Herod's Temple in Jesus' day were so carefully cut,
shaped, and prepared in advance at the quarries that they were
simply set or slid into place without the use of any metal
tools! They had to be because the sound of metal hammers,
chisels, or any other iron instrument was strictly forbidden in
the vicinity of the Temple. In other words, the Temple site
was already considered holy and sacred (set apart) to God—
even before the first stone was laid.

Another interpretation might be that the House of the
Spirit was already preexistent in the Kingdom of God, so the
building of the physical representation of the spiritual reality
was to be constructed in a godly hush and awe. Our temples
are still "building" and being transformed from glory to glory,
but from the very beginning we are warned that our bodies are
the temples of God. Above all, the true apostle of God *must*
be gifted with the wisdom of God because we are told in
Proverbs 9:1, "Wisdom hath builded her house."

Apostles Are Pioneers

Yea, so have I strived to preach the gospel, not where Christ was named, lest I should build upon another man's foundation: but as it is written, To whom he was not spoken of, they shall see: and they that have not heard shall understand (Romans 15:20-21).

A *pioneer* is "a member of a military unit usually of construction engineers," and "one of the first to settle in a territory." To *pioneer* is "to open or prepare for others to follow, also, settle. To originate or take part in the development of."[1] Another definition says a pioneer "opens a way or originates, an explorer, one of an advance body clearing or repairing a road for troops or foot soldiers."

According to the New Testament record, Paul established churches in four provinces of the Roman Empire: Galatia, Macedonia, Achaia, and Asia. After these works were established, he turned his attention to the west. The only way we can fulfill the great commission is for us to recapture the apostolic pioneering spirit that motivated Paul to pour out his life for the gospel. It is this supernatural spirit that will move us out of our comfort zones to bring Christ to unreached people groups.

When the great commission is spearheaded and propelled forward with an apostolic spirit, it will produce nothing less than world-changing, generation-wide evangelization. Paul and the twelve apostles evangelized much of the known world in their day; Paul covered all of what was then called Asia in only three years.

The primary mission of apostles is to preach the gospel, convert people to Christ, and plant churches. The pioneering apostolic anointing is a *breakthrough anointing* that advances the Church into new regions where the gospel has never been preached before. Pioneers are the first to get there. They have an inner drive to accomplish new things, and like the apostle Paul, they do not want to build on someone else's foundation.

An apostolic pioneer's anointing and ambition is to preach the gospel where Christ is not known or where His light is dim. "New conquests for Christ!" is the heart-cry of every apostolic pioneer:

> *Blessed are those whose strength is in you, who have set their hearts on pilgrimage. As they pass through the Valley of Baca, they make it a place of springs; the autumn rains also cover it with pools. They go from strength to strength, till each appears before God in Zion* (Psalm 84:5-7 NIV).

> *But we will not boast of things without our measure, but according to the measure of the rule which God hath distributed to us, a measure to reach even unto you* (2 Corinthians 10:13).

Apostles Are Commissioned Ones

Apostles are "sent ones," which means they are sent to do something by someone who sent them. Every true apostle—regardless of type or level of authority—has both a supernatural call and a commission.

1. Jesus was **called** and **sent** by the heavenly Father.

> *But I have greater witness than that of John: for the works which the Father hath given me to finish, the same works that I do, bear witness of me, that the Father hath sent me. And the Father himself, which hath sent me, hath borne witness of me. Ye have neither heard his voice at any time, nor seen his shape* (John 5:36-37).

2. The twelve "apostles of the Lamb" were **chosen** and **sent** (ordained or "set in place") by Jesus.

> *Ye have not chosen me, but I have chosen you, and ordained you, that ye should go and bring forth fruit, and that your fruit should remain: that whatsoever ye shall ask of the Father in my name, he may give it you* (John 15:16).

3. Paul was **called**, but not by the will of man.

> *Paul, called to be an apostle of Jesus Christ through the will of God, and Sosthenes our brother* (1 Corinthians 1:1).

> *Paul, an apostle of Jesus Christ by the will of God, and Timothy our brother* (2 Corinthians 1:1).

4. Jesus **commissioned** His disciples as the first apostles to act on His behalf and to use His authority (*all* authority) to make disciples of all nations and to plant churches throughout the known world.

> *Now then we are ambassadors for Christ, as though God did beseech you by us: we pray you in Christ's stead, be ye reconciled to God* (2 Corinthians 5:20).

> *And Jesus came and spake unto them, saying, All power is given unto me in heaven and in earth. Go ye therefore, and teach all nations, baptizing them in the name of the Father, and of the Son, and of the Holy Ghost: teaching them to observe all things whatsoever I have commanded you: and, lo, I am with you alway, even unto the end of the world. Amen* (Matthew 28:18-20).

> *These twelve Jesus sent forth, and commanded them, saying, Go not into the way of the Gentiles, and into any city of the Samaritans enter ye not: but*

go rather to the lost sheep of the house of Israel. And as ye go, preach, saying, The kingdom of heaven is at hand (Matthew 10:5-7).

5. Saul of Tarsus, later called Paul, was first called as an apostle by direct revelation of Jesus Christ. Then he was sent and commissioned by the apostles of the Lamb.

> *And I said, Who art thou, Lord? And he said, I am Jesus whom thou persecutest. But rise, and stand upon thy feet: for I have appeared unto thee for this purpose, to make thee a minister and a witness both of these things which thou hast seen, and of those things in the which I will appear unto thee; delivering thee from the people, and from the Gentiles, unto whom now I send thee, to open their eyes, and to turn them from darkness to light, and from the power of Satan unto God, that they may receive forgiveness of sins, and inheritance among them which are sanctified by faith that is in me* (Acts 26:15-18).

> *As they ministered to the Lord, and fasted, the Holy Ghost said, Separate me Barnabas and Saul for the work whereunto I have called them. And when they had fasted and prayed, and laid their hands on them, they sent them away. So they, being sent forth by the Holy Ghost, departed...* (Acts 13:2-4).

Paul was given a specific work and was commissioned to...
- Open their eyes.
- Turn them from darkness to light.
- Turn them from the power of Satan to God.

Paul's call was very similar to the ancient call of Jesus Christ as Messiah. His commission was rooted in the Father's revelation to the prophet Isaiah, which was quoted by Luke the physician in his Gospel:

The Spirit of the Lord is upon me, because he hath anointed me to preach the gospel to the poor; he hath sent me to heal the brokenhearted, to preach deliverance to the captives, and recovering of sight to the blind, to set at liberty them that are bruised, to preach the acceptable year of the Lord (Luke 4:18-19).

Jesus was commissioned to...
- Preach the gospel to the poor.
- Heal the brokenhearted.
- Preach deliverance to the captives.
- Preach recovery of sight to the blind.
- Set at liberty those who are oppressed.
- Preach the acceptable year of the Lord.

The call and ministry of apostles today have several things in common with those of the apostles of the Lamb and of Paul:

1. Apostleship is not based on gifts. Rather, it is based on divine call and commission. (See Matthew 28.)
2. It is not based on human qualifications but on divine commission. No one should assume the function of an apostle simply because he has the required gifts or ability.
3. Only God's will and call constitutes apostleship.
4. Paul's call came directly from the Lord, "one on one," while his separation and "sending" was a corporate action done at the command of the Holy Spirit. Paul's call, as with those of modern-day apostles, was recognized and publicly confirmed

17

and affirmed by other *doma* or ascension leadership gifts within the Body of Christ (i.e., prophets and teachers). Paul was "set apart" from the local body of believers to be "sent out" for a specific task. This is also the case with many apostles today.

5. The "credentials" of apostolic ministries are the transformed lives of the people they bring to Christ, the churches they plant, and the leaders they produce to lead those churches. You can know an "apostle" by the fruit of his ministry. (Read First Corinthians 9:1-2, where Paul says, "...the seal of mine apostleship are ye in the Lord.")

6. A commission carries with it the full authority of the commissioning power or entity. A police officer carries the full authority of the local government and community he serves. An apostle carries the full authority of the Head of the Church to make disciples of all nations and to preach the gospel *with signs following* (Mark 16:20).

Endnote

1. *Webster's Ninth New Collegiate Dictionary* (Springfield, MA: Merriam-Webster Inc., Publishers, 1991), 894.

Chapter 3

Apostolic Churches

There is a new breed of men and women emerging in the earth today. They are a "new breed" not by virtue of their birth, education, or personality type; but rather by their new birth, by their spiritual discernment, and by God's divine call and plan. They are unwilling to become complacent settlers and conformists. This new company of people is determined to serve their generation by openly revealing and modeling God's purposes in the earth for this day.

This apostolic band of radical reformers and pioneers is crafting and redesigning a new brand of Church life based on an ancient dream of God. They are refocusing the people and resources of the Church to finish the task of world evangelization and to lift Jesus higher than every obstacle and dividing wall. This apostolic company of pioneers that is being restored to the Church has a burning passion to advance the Kingdom of the living God into new spiritual territories and positions of victory.

God, by His Spirit, has called this apostolic company of men and women into being to fulfill His desire to form a people who are conformed to and modeled after Christ, the Great Apostle of our faith. This has been accomplished in part as a result of a great apostolic movement that God has raised up in the earth this day.

This apostolic movement, and the company of apostolic churches it has birthed or identified, have similar apostolic patterns, trends, governmental styles, and operating principles that guide their behavior. It can essentially be boiled down to four words: They *think*, *pray*, *give*, and *go*. This apostolic people exhibits a mind-set much like the apostolic culture of the Church in the Book of Acts in the first century. If we take a close look at Acts 13, we will discover one of the key characteristics of the church at Antioch in Paul's day.

Now there were in the church that was at Antioch certain prophets and teachers; as Barnabas, and Simeon that was called Niger, and Lucius of Cyrene, and Manaen, which had been brought up with Herod the tetrarch, and Saul (Acts 13:1).

Cultural Diversity

The leaders in the church at Antioch represented an extraordinary collection of diverse backgrounds. Niger means black in Latin, the mother tongue of ancient Rome. Lucius of Cyrene came from a leading city in North Africa in what is now Libya. Manaen was from the most privileged ranks of society in Israel, having grown up with Herod Antipas, then the ruler of the "Palestine" region under Caesar. Saul of Tarsus was a Jew, a Pharisee with impeccable training and credentials (before Christ), and a Roman citizen by birth.

For there is no difference between the Jew and the Greek... (Romans 10:12).

And have put on the new man, which is renewed in knowledge after the image of him that created him: where there is neither Greek nor Jew, circumcision nor uncircumcision, Barbarian, Scythian, bond nor free: but Christ is all, and in all (Colossians 3:10-11).

None of these men in Antioch were limited or confined to their "natural" or earthly station as defined by race, social status, economic background, or education. They all became or made up the "holy nation" of God described by the apostle Peter:

But ye are a chosen generation, a royal priesthood, an holy nation, a peculiar people; that ye should show forth the praises of him who hath called you out of darkness into his marvellous light (1 Peter 2:9).

Like the leaders at Antioch, we have changed our citizenship through Christ Jesus and have become a holy nation unto God. The Greek word for "nation" is *ethnos*. This is the word from which we derive our English word *ethnic*. The church at Antioch evidently understood that the Church of God is a heavenly nation planted among the earthbound nations of the world.

In a very real sense, the church at Antioch more accurately represents God's greater will for the Church than the predominately Jewish church at Jerusalem. No, this has nothing to do with the racial mixture or predominate race or culture in these cities *per se*, but with the *obedience* of the respective churches to the vision and direct commands of Christ. In fact, there is a clear contrast between the "Jerusalem mentality" and the "Antioch mentality."

Jesus personally delivered "the great commisssion," the final marching orders, to the people who would lead the Church at Jerusalem after it was "born in a day" on the Day

21

of Pentecost. Moments before He ascended into Heaven, Jesus told the disciples—and the Church that would follow after them:

> *Afterward he appeared unto the eleven as they sat at meat, and upbraided them with their unbelief and hardness of heart, because they believed not them which had seen him after he was risen. And he said unto them, **Go ye** into **all the world**, and preach the gospel to **every creature*** (Mark 16:14-15).

Three problems quickly showed up in the Jerusalem church that are directly related to Jesus' words in this passage. First, the Christian believers in Jerusalem generally preferred *not to go anywhere* outside of their city—they seemed to expect everyone to come to them instead. Second, when they did venture out into "the world" with the gospel, they tended to confine their outreach to the "Jewish" world, not the world as a whole.

Third, and somewhat related to the second problem, is, when the believers in Jerusalem did finally begin to preach to or accept non-Jewish converts to Christ, they tended to preach a special "Jewish gospel." What they preached included the doctrine of the cross *plus* rigid dietary and religious rules of levitical law—including the requirement that all male Gentile believers be circumcised.

It doesn't take much imagination to hear similar things about the established Church today! We expect people to come to us instead of us going to them. We spend most of our time and resources reaching and ministering to Christians instead of to the lost, and, finally, when we do manage to go out into the "world," we like to teach a modified gospel. We often demand that converts first look, act, and talk like us *before* we accept them into the fold.

Racial and cultural prejudice are ancient problems. The predominately Jewish congregation in Jerusalem had a serious racial prejudice problem. They didn't like to fellowship with Gentiles, especially if those Gentiles refused to become Jewish in their customs, attire, and worship patterns. It seems that the church at Jerusalem had no intention of fulfilling the great commission. They seemed to be quite content to stay in Jerusalem until the Lord returned, and for all intents and purposes, they were a "Jews only" church.

The first deacons were appointed to correct unfair treatment of non-Jewish widows in the first church benevolence program (see Acts 6:1). In the end, God had to catapult the Jewish church out of Jerusalem through persecution to transform those believers into apostolic people.

The term "Christians" was first coined in the multi-cultural setting of Antioch. The church at Antioch, unlike the temple-based congregation at Jerusalem, was a multi-cultural, multinational apostolic company that could not be contained by the hindering walls of racism. It seemed to exemplify the Body of Christ described by Paul the apostle in his letter to the Colossians: "Where there is neither Greek nor Jew, circumcision nor uncircumcision, Barbarian, Scythian, bond nor free: but Christ is all, and in all" (Col. 3:11).

The Antioch church seemed to have no class, gender, economic, racial, or educational limitations. The believers in Antioch seemed to understand the concept of the "holy nation" and a "peculiar" (or "purchased and wrapped around"[1]) people set apart unto God described in Peter's Epistle (see 1 Pet. 2:9). It should be no surprise to us that the Spirit of God is birthing an Antioch model of apostolic churches and people around the world.

The original apostolic band gathered around Jesus Christ was composed of people from widely different groups and identities. The Lord's apostles included Simon Peter, a former Zealot (a terrorist/anti-Roman extremist), and Matthew, a former "publican" or tax collector.

Now the names of the twelve apostles are these; The first, Simon, who is called Peter, and Andrew his brother; James the son of Zebedee, and John his brother; Philip, and Bartholomew; Thomas, and Matthew the publican; James the son of Alphaeus, and Lebbaeus, whose surname was Thaddaeus; Simon the Canaanite, and Judas Iscariot, who also betrayed him (Matthew 10:2-4).

No one despised the publicans more than the Zealots, for publicans were seen to be collaborators with the hated Romans. Yet in Christ, these two adversaries were reconciled. Fellowship even extended to the Samaritans (see Acts 8), the "half-Jewish" people who had been rejected by Jews for centuries. The Church crossed the barriers of worldly society and welcomed even these ancient outcasts into the fellowship of the saints.

Acts 10 shows us that it was very difficult for Peter to receive and fellowship with Gentiles. Cornelius was a Roman, and a centurion or captain of 100 elite Roman soldiers (and thus the stereotypical symbol of oppression in the eyes of the Jews).

God's Call Falls on *Women* Too

These all continued with one accord in prayer and supplication, with the women, and Mary the mother of Jesus, and with his brethren (Acts 1:14).

And on my servants and on my handmaidens I will pour out in those days of My Spirit; and they shall prophesy (Acts 2:18).

Women were among those who were filled with the Holy Spirit, in fulfillment of ancient prophecy. It is clear that the early Church recognized and respected God's call upon the lives of women. For instance, the Bible record specifically tells us that Paul and his apostolic company stayed as guests in the home of Philip the evangelist in Caesarea and that Philip had four daughters who prophesied (see Acts 21:8-9). This and many other New Testament references from Paul and the other writers make it clear that women were an integral part of the gospel.

Apostolic Churches Appreciate Diversity

And the day following Paul went in with us unto James; and all the elders were present. And when he had saluted them, he declared particularly what things God had wrought among the Gentiles by his ministry. And when they heard it, they glorified the Lord (Acts 21:18-20a).

Now there were in the church that was at Antioch certain prophets and teachers; as Barnabas, and Simeon that was called Niger, and Lucius of Cyrene, and Manaen, which had been brought up with Herod the tetrarch, and Saul (Acts 13:1).

As mentioned earlier, the Book of Acts records an amazingly diverse list of leaders in the church at Antioch. They came from a wide variety of social, ethnic, and linguistic backgrounds, yet they and the church in Antioch seemed to be at ease with all the different cultures represented there—most likely because of the love of Christ in their hearts. Lucius of Cyrene was one of the leaders of the church there. This is significant because Cyrene was the capital of Libya, strongly implying that Lucius was a black man from North Africa.

On the Day of Pentecost described in Acts 2, men and women from diverse linguistic and cultural backgrounds, including bondmen and free men, were filled with the Holy Spirit in Jerusalem. This diversity was due mostly to the fact that it was the high holy day when every Jewish male was required by Jewish law to come to Jerusalem. So even though the crowd was diverse, it was still mostly Jewish. Antioch, however, was a multi-cultural society composed mostly of Gentile and pagan peoples.

The church at Antioch—as an apostolic church—brought forth and pioneered trans-cultural truths from the Scriptures, separated them from the irrelevant cultural applications of previous eras, and successfully applied them to their own relevant culture. These biblical principles work in every culture because they are eternal, just as their Originator is eternal.

It was in Antioch that the ancient cultural barrier between Jew and Gentile was broken down and replaced with unity in the Son of God. As the Scriptures tell us:

Wherefore remember, that ye being in time past Gentiles in the flesh, who are called Uncircumcision by that which is called the Circumcision in the flesh made by hands...But now in Christ Jesus ye who sometimes were far off are made nigh by the blood of Christ. For he is our peace, who hath made both one, and hath broken down the middle wall of partition between us...that he might reconcile both unto God in one body by the cross, having slain the enmity thereby (Ephesians 2:11,13-14,16).

It was God's plan and glory to bring a rich diversity of cultures, races, and social strata together at the same time under one banner and Savior to enjoy unity and the uniqueness of one another as His chosen people. It is as this apostolic company that we truly bear His image and likeness through the cross and through our willingness to relate in true fellowship (or *koinonia* in the Greek). John Webster wrote in the book, *Making Christ Known*:

> "The attempt to impose another culture on people who have their own is cultural imperialism. The preservation of cultural diversity honors God, respects man, enriches life, and promotes evangelization. Each church, if it is to be truly indigenous, should be rooted in the soil of its local culture."[2]

Apostolic Churches Minister to the Lord First

True apostolic assemblies of believers are characterized by their abiding commitment to worship, praise, prayer, intercession, and spiritual warfare. They are worshiping bodies and conquering armies assembled under the banner of the living and holy God.

> *Now there were in the church that was at Antioch certain prophets and teachers; as Barnabas, and Simeon that was called Niger, and Lucius of Cyrene, and Manaen, which had been brought up with Herod the tetrarch, and Saul. **As they ministered to the Lord, and fasted**, the Holy Ghost said, Separate me Barnabas and Saul for the work whereunto I have called them* (Acts 13:1-2).

God has always separated ministers unto Himself. In the Old Testament, the prophet Ezekiel described three levels of priests who functioned before the Lord and the children of Israel. The two lower groups of priests were responsible for the daily priestly duties in the outer court and in the holy place of the Temple, but were not allowed to minister before God's *shekinah* glory because they had not been separated or sanctified. Their wrong choices had defiled and disqualified them.

Yet they shall be ministers in my sanctuary, having charge at the gates of the house, and ministering to the house: they shall slay the burnt offering and the sacrifice for the people, and they shall stand before them to minister unto them (Ezekiel 44:11).

The lowest level of the priesthood included certain priests who had strayed from the Lord at some time in their lives, stooping so low as to offer sacrifices to the popular gods that the Israelites had "borrowed" from the neighboring lands. These priests were more interested in pleasing the people than in pleasing God Almighty.

Because they ministered unto them before their idols, and caused the house of Israel to fall into iniquity; therefore have I lifted up mine hand against them, saith the Lord God, and they shall bear their iniquity. And they shall not come near unto me, to do the office of a priest unto me, nor to come near to any of my holy things, in the most holy place: but they shall bear their shame, and their abominations which they have committed. But I will make them keepers of the charge of the house, for all the service thereof, and for all that shall be done therein (Ezekiel 44:12-14).

These disqualified priests ministered in the sanctuary and as gatekeepers of the house of the Lord. They were given the mundane and primarily physical work of slaying the burnt offerings and offering the minor sacrifices for the people. Their ministry was to the people more than to God, and it was their wayward leadership that had caused God's people to fall into iniquity (or lawlessness). Now their sin had banished them to the "outer court," separated from the holy Presence of God in the Most Holy Place.

We have the same kind of "priests" among us today. Yet God always has a remnant preserved and set aside unto Himself, and it is this kind of priest and servant that He is beginning to reveal today.

*But the priests the Levites, the sons of Zadok, that kept the charge of my sanctuary when the children of Israel went astray from me, **they shall come near to me** to minister unto me, and **they shall stand before me** to offer unto me the fat and the blood, saith the Lord God. They shall **enter into my sanctuary**, and they shall **come near** to my table, **to minister unto me**, and they shall keep my charge* (Ezekiel 44:15-16).

The third and highest level of priests were taken from the sons of Zadok (which means "just"). Zadok was the high priest under King David when all of Judah rose up against him after being deceived by Absalom, David's rebellious son. Zadok dared to remain in Jerusalem faithfully attending to the Lord and staying loyal to the king while all of Israel turned away from God and King David in anger.

When King David was forced to flee Jerusalem and Absalom's armies for a time, Zadok obediently returned the Ark of the Covenant to the city and continued to fill the Tabernacle of David with psalms, spiritual songs, and worship just as he had been taught by King David's prophetic New Testament example for decades.

God is calling into existence an apostolic Zadok company of people to worship before the Lord in our day as well. Worship is important to every generation because it crafts an atmosphere that welcomes and honors the presence of the Lord in the midst of the Church. Yet it is especially important in our day because of the magnitude of God's visitation across the earth. This apostolic Zadok company of fearless worshipers is destined to play a key role in the pioneering, soul-winning, disciple-making flood of God's power in this generation.

Endnotes

1. Drawn from definitions from the Greek found in James Strong, *Strong's Exhaustive Concordance of the Bible* (Peabody, MA: Hendrickson Publishers, n.d.), **peculiar** (Greek, #4047, 4046).
2. John Webster, *Making Christ Known*, 63.

Chapter 4

Apostolic Churches, Corporate Worship, and Team Ministry

It is no accident that music and worship are becoming more artistic with skillful, creative, and spontaneous singing before the Lord. God is using this kind of anointed worship and adoration to produce and inspire an apostolic people with enthusiasm and vibrancy.

Meanwhile the spirit of religion and tradition has also risen up to kill, stifle, or limit the innovative and creative work of the Holy Spirit among people in our day. In the very face of this rising opposition, the apostolic company of worshipers called by God into leadership is pioneering new depths of the Spirit and creating a *new sound* of worship. This too is no accident. Every season or movement of God has a new and fresh sound.

Through the guidance and encouragement of sensitive leadership, these apostolic people are crafting a lifestyle of worship of divine design that is perfectly made to be "taken to the streets"! Although worship is a matter of the heart and an expression of our inner relationship with God, it is also meant to be a public expression of our corporate relationship with God.

Worship First, Works Second

*And Jesus answered and said to her, "Martha, **Martha, you are worried and troubled** about many things. But one thing is needed, and **Mary has chosen that good part**, which will not be taken away from her"* (Luke 10:41-42 NKJV).

Martha and Mary both loved the Lord Jesus. Martha was concerned with her work for the Master, especially the preparation of the food and tables. Her concern became so overpowering that Martha interrupted the Lord to complain that her sister, Mary, did not care about the work. Jesus' answer should become the *modus operandi*, the way of life, for everyone in God's last-days apostolic company.

Jesus said that Mary had chosen the better part when she decided to stay positioned at His feet, soaking in His presence and His every word and movement. This "better part" choice can never be taken away. The Lord wants us to have Mary's type of relationship with Him as *the Lord of the work* instead of Martha's type with religious activities—*the work of the Lord*. We must put the Lord first, knowing that the work will proceed naturally and supernaturally out of our vital relationship with Him. May we never be too busy, like Martha, to cease from our labors and listen exclusively to the Master's still small voice.

The primary focus of the church in Antioch was worship unto the Lord. In other words, the dominant and most vital New Testament Church, the congregation at Antioch, was a worship center *first* and a work and missionary center second. After that apostolic company ministered to the Lord in worship and feasted on His Word, the Holy Spirit gave specific "work directions" and issued commissions of power for the saints. It is in the midst of worship that we find the Holy Spirit moving in the midst of believers.

The Apostolic Church Practices Team Ministry

*Now there were in the church that was at Antioch **certain prophets and teachers**; as Barnabas, and Simeon that was called Niger, and Lucius of Cyrene, and Manaen, which had been brought up with Herod the tetrarch, and Saul. As they ministered to the Lord, and fasted, the Holy Ghost said, **Separate me Barnabas and Saul for the work** whereunto I have called them* (Acts 13:1-2).

The fledgling church at Antioch had a team of gifted people, including teachers, prophets, and apostles, who functioned together to minister to the Lord through prayer and fasting. As a result, the most dynamic evangelistic and apostolic church-planting team ever assembled was unleashed upon the earth.

A new apostolic company of leaders in our day is being raised up in preparation for God's great harvest movement in the earth. He is rapidly restoring and activating all the supernatural *charis* or grace gifts (see 1 Cor. 12) and leadership or *doma* gifts lying dormant within the Body of Christ.

What is His goal? To see "...the whole body fitly joined together and compacted by that which every joint supplieth, according to the effectual working in the measure of every part, maketh increase of the body unto the edifying of itself in love" (Eph. 4:16).

Christ Ordained a Body, Not Superstars

For as the body is one, and hath many members, and all the members of that one body, being many, are one body; so also is Christ (1 Corinthians 12:12).

Deacons, elders, bishops, pastors, teachers, evangelists, prophets, and apostles are all coming together into a mature man to the stature of Christ (see Eph. 4:13). Gone are the days of "lone rangers" packing a "superstar mentality" and wielding a death grip on the affections of many in the Church. The apostolic church body is a functioning *team*, a body united around the Risen Christ who *alone* is worthy of the glory.

The Apostolic Vision: To Come, Impart, and Establish

*Making request, if by any means now at length I might have a prosperous journey by the will of God **to come** unto you. For I long to see you, that I may **impart unto you** some spiritual gift, to the end ye may **be established*** (Romans 1:10-11).

The apostles of the first century Church had no limitations concerning their scope of ministry (other than what God told them to do or not to do). They were not bound by geographical, national, or cultural boundaries. They had received and believed a God-given vision and command directly from the Risen Lord that the gospel was to go to every people and nation, even to the uttermost ends of the earth. What we see in Matthew 28 is the Head of the Church imparting a world vision to the first local church.

The church at Antioch had developed a foreign policy and global vision that was clearly demonstrated in their apostolic prayer meetings, where the leaders interceded in prayer for doors to open in regions where the gospel had never been preached.

When the doors opened, they sent their best men and women to new territories and fields to plant, water, and reap a harvest. Their mission was long-term and far-reaching in scope. They went to establish permanent, indigenous local churches in suburbs, cities, nations, and communities among all the known people groups of the earth.

Its members and leaders selflessly gave of themselves and of their talents. They prayed, sent, went, and gave of their resources. The care of the existing and young churches were daily on the hearts of the apostles. The apostle Paul wrote, "Besides the other things, what comes upon me daily: my *deep concern* for all the churches" (2 Cor. 11:28 NKJV).

The Apostolic Church Is a Training Center

Wherefore I put thee in remembrance that thou stir up the gift of God, which is in thee by the putting on of my hands (2 Timothy 1:6).

For I long to see you, that I may impart unto you some spiritual gift, to the end ye may be established (Romans 1:11).

Apostolic churches are to be training schools and schools of the Spirit where revelation knowledge is shared and understood, and where gifts are imparted, activated, trained up, and commissioned. For the most part, we think too small as Christians. Paul tried to help us break out of our limitations when he wrote:

But as it is written, Eye hath not seen, nor ear heard, neither have entered into the heart of man, the things which God hath prepared for them that love him. But God hath revealed them unto us by his Spirit: for the

Spirit searcheth all things, yea, the deep things of God
(1 Corinthians 2:9-10).

The biblical mode of training does not consist merely of the transfer of information on an intellectual level; it involves the much deeper process of spiritual impartation. Jesus, Barnabas, and Paul the apostle all used the long-term method of *discipleship* to raise up leaders to follow in their footsteps, and they managed to turn the world upside down in the process.

There are other ways to impart spiritual gifts or deposits as well. For instance, Paul said that he longed to impart spiritual gifts to the saints in Rome (see Rom. 1:11). This type of impartation came through the laying on of hands and through the apostles speaking in and through the Holy Spirit and wisdom. The same thing happens today through the biblical operation of the *charis* or grace gifts listed by Paul in First Corinthians 12.

Jesus Himself imparted five key "equipping gifts" for permanent service to the Church as long as the Bride of Christ is in need of training, instruction, and direction in the work of the ministry and the path of perfection.

And he gave some, apostles; and some, prophets; and some, evangelists; and some, pastors and teachers; for the perfecting of the saints, for the work of the ministry, for the edifying of the body of Christ: till we all come in the unity of the faith, and of the knowledge of the Son of God, unto a perfect man, unto the measure of the stature of the fulness of Christ (Ephesians 4:11-13).

It is through these living gifts imparted to men and women called to leadership that the saints are equipped with the Word. The job of these ascension gifts is to help identify and confirm the call and gifts resident in each believer and to train and release them to their God-given call or work.

The Apostolic Church Is a "Sending" Church

In accordance with the exhortation in Hebrews 6 for God's people to go on past the basic principles of the faith, the true apostolic church lays hands on qualified candidates and sends them out as an apostolic people to finish the task of global evangelism. Every member in the ideal apostolic company will understand their measure or grace and fully function in their respective calls, gifts, and functions in the Church.

The Apostolic Church Is a Resource Center

Then the disciples, every man according to his ability, determined to send relief unto the brethren which dwelt in Judaea: which also they did, and sent it to the elders by the hands of Barnabas and Saul (Acts 11:29-30).

It was at this point in the life of the church at Antioch, when Agabus the prophet foretold the soon-coming persecution that would fall upon Jerusalem, that *the saints in Antioch did for their brethren in Jerusalem what the Jerusalem believers did for others in the beginning*: They sold possessions such as lands and houses and laid the money at the apostles' feet for distribution to those in need (see Acts 4:33-35).

This is the true apostolic heart—caring for the churches and brethren in need; faithfully distributing money and needed manpower in ministry; and conducting unceasing intercessory prayer for the network of churches.

It is the mark of an apostolic church that the people *give more than they use on themselves*. When they pray, they effectively mobilize angels through their fervency and unity of heart, and they regularly receive *answers* to their prayers.

37

As a resource center, an apostolic church will typically have an overabundance of ministry resources available. Most apostolic congregations have a high percentage of "called-out, fivefold ministries" in their meetings—but they don't tend to stay inactive for long periods. They are often sent out in "apostolic teams" for church planting and training missions to raise up new elders and leaders "in the field."

The ministry gifts representing apostolic churches are kept busy because their sending congregation is considered by other churches, ministries, and saints to be their place of refuge, strength, example, and apostolic supply. They serve as models for others.

> *Whether any do inquire of Titus, he is my partner and fellowhelper concerning you: or our brethren be inquired of, they are the messengers of the churches, and the glory of Christ* (2 Corinthians 8:23).

Collections are often received from apostolic churches to feed and clothe poor brethren in an entirely different location or culture. Paul told the believers at Philippi, "Yet I supposed it necessary to send to you Epaphroditus, my brother, and companion in labour, and fellowsoldier, but your messenger, and he that ministered to my wants" (Phil. 2:25).

Apostolic churches constantly pray for the direction and supernatural supply of their apostolic teams, because evangelism was considered a *team ministry*. The sending church paves the way in prayer while the sent ones simply obey God's leading and go.

One of the most remarkable things about the New Testament Church of the first century was that Paul and the churches labored in *partnership* in the gospel. They freely shared their resources to proclaim the gospel of Jesus Christ to all of the world.

Chapter 5

Apostles and Apostolic Congregations

In a sense, "success" is one of the greatest threats to genuine apostolic authority and ministry in the modern Church. I say this because success, or prominent visible fruit, draws attention. Attention attracts the attention of others who *seek* attention. These attention seekers are all too quick to "codify, package, and market" anything that "works."

The reason that the office of apostle and the making of what I call an "apostolic people" cannot be packaged and "mass marketed" is simple: They aren't for sale, and they cannot be programmed or duplicated outside of God-ordained relationships and God's grace.

An apostle does not relate to a local church through some official authority structure "voted on" or "dictated" by some board of ecclesiastical masters or apostles. All men can do is simply recognize what God has already done in a person and a people. This is very similar to the way the Holy Spirit distributed *charis* or "grace gifts" to individual members of the Church, "...dividing to every man severally *as he wills*" (1 Cor. 12:11).

Apostolic authority is *spiritual* authority, and it does not carry with it the right or authority to conduct a dictatorship of any kind, nor does it authorize an apostle or apostolic impostor to "lord it over" God's precious heritage. Equally important, true apostolic authority is never "assumed" authority created and preserved through presumption. Genuine apostolic authority is *earned* and maintained by mutual covenant relationship.

Apostleship Does Not Mean "Control"

> *Not that we lord it over your faith, but **we work with you** for your joy, because it is by faith you stand firm* (2 Corinthians 1:24 NIV).

Paul, as the "founding apostle" of the church at Corinth, told the believers there that he did not control or "lord it over" their faith. He chose instead to minister to them as a loving father would work with his children for their joy. (Paul was their "father in the faith" since he founded the church, led many if not most of them to the Lord, and provided most of their training and discipleship.)

Apostles who travel through and minister to a network of churches must respect the authority of local churches, particularly the authority of the senior elder and elder/leadership team within a local church. By network I mean "family." For instance, in my family "network," I am the father of my children, the husband of my wife, and the head of my home. However, I cannot assume or usurp headship over my brother's wife and his children as well. At the invitation of my brother, I can speak into the life of his family, but even then it must be with respect for his authority. The same protocol demands that I function ethically to the extended family of God.

Two Levels of Relationship

Apostles today generally have two levels of relationship in their ministries. The first level involves an ongoing relationship with "spiritual sons" who have been raised up in the local church. These are his personal sons whom he has personally trained and equipped for the ministry of the gospel in his stead. They are the "fruit" of his ministry and the duplication of his call.

The apostle is a "father" to these individuals. They have come to know his apostolic patterns and are an extension of the local church body he serves, as well as of his apostolic ministry received from God. This relationship exists because the apostle has carefully invested himself in his spiritual "sons" as a discipler and father in the faith.[1] We see this in Jesus' relationship with the twelve disciples, in Barnabas' early relationship with Paul, and later in Paul's relationship with Timothy, John Mark, Titus, and many others.

The second level of relationship concerns the apostle's responsibility to relate to those who are a part of the larger church network. This includes individuals and local church bodies who have felt the need for apostolic relationship and sought the apostle's counsel and advice. These individuals and church bodies may have already established their own ministry patterns, thus requiring a less intense level of relationship, interaction, and accountability with the apostle.

The apostle Paul was clearly demonstrating the difference between his first level relationship with the Corinthians and his second level relationships with believers in some other places when he told the Corinthian believers, "If I be not an apostle unto others, yet doubtless I am to you..." (1 Cor. 9:2).

The Apostles' Accountability to Local Churches

So they, being sent forth by the Holy Ghost, departed unto Seleucia; and from thence they sailed to Cyprus. And when they were at Salamis, they preached the word of God in the synagogues of the Jews: and they had also John to their minister. And when they had gone through the isle unto Paphos, they found a certain sorcerer, a false prophet, a Jew, whose name was Barjesus (Acts 13:4-6).

The New Testament, and the Book of Acts in particular, tells us that the apostles in the first century were commissioned and *sent out* by the Holy Spirit and by the leadership gifts in local churches. With the blessing and support of these local congregations, the apostles traveled by road and by sea to found new churches in Iconium, Lystra, and Derbe (Acts 14:1,6-7,19).

The Holy Spirit was the first and primary guide governing the movement of the apostles in the New Testament. God also spoke to the early apostles and church leaders through divinely orchestrated relationships with other people (or "Kingdom connections"), visions, and angelic visitations, imparting guidance and direction.

Long-Term Apostolic Relationships

True apostles never abandon the works they establish, just as true parents will never abandon the children they bring into this world. Throughout the Book of Acts and the Epistles, we see apostles going to great lengths and often facing great danger to themselves to return to the churches they founded to *strengthen* them. This involved the work of confirming, supporting, instructing, and correcting new believers to firmly establish them in their new faith in the midst of often hostile circumstances.

In most cases, once the apostles of the New Testament fulfilled their respective missions, they returned to the apostolic center from which they were sent out or had been committed to the grace of God. In most cases, they gave the brethren an account of their work in private and public gatherings. This pattern of willing submission and relationship to "sending bodies" is a lesson we need to learn today.

All ministries and ministers in particular must be accountable to the local church from which they are sent. This is for their own protection and safety! The inherent isolation common to the apostolic, prophetic, and evangelistic traveling ministries poses a unique danger for Christian leaders, and they have a vital need for input and accountability to other brethren whom they respect and love.

Frankly, I've seen some very strange practices going on in the Body of Christ today, and in virtually every case, the people responsible for introducing, promoting, or condoning these practices were not being held accountable to anyone for their lifestyle, ministry, or character.

Those with only a casual knowledge of the Scriptures might be tempted to think that the apostle Paul was a loner or an independent apostle who was aloof from the "apostles of the Lamb" based in Jerusalem. The Scriptures simply do not support this idea. On one occasion, Paul specifically made a trip to Jerusalem to "double check" his doctrine with Peter and the other apostles at Jerusalem (see Gal. 2:1-2).

And how shall they preach, except they be sent? as it is written, How beautiful are the feet of them that preach the gospel of peace, and bring glad tidings of good things! (Romans 10:15).

Beware the "Lone Ranger" Syndrome

The apostolic arena is also subject to the error I call "the Lone Ranger" syndrome, named after the "outlaw" peace officer of American TV fame who fought outlaws and crime in the Old West frontier while wearing a mask and reporting to no one. Many serious problems in the Church have been created or made worse by the actions of "Lone Ranger" apostles who "went without being sent."

Two of the most important laws of leadership in God's Kingdom are that "the greatest must be the servant of all" and that "the disciple is not greater than his Teacher" (see Matt. 23:11; John 13:16). It is God's plan for leaders to first learn how to be followers. Those who would give orders or instruction must first learn to receive and follow orders themselves. Military leaders of every generation have known the truth that the best generals were those who learned how to follow orders and do their duty regardless of adversity or circumstances— *before* they achieved high rank.

As this apostolic move grows in the earth, we are going to see the misinformed pictures we have of leadership, leaders, and leadership structure readjusted in the Body. The simple fact is that apostles today, as in the first century, are not above accountability and discipline.

The great Apostle of our faith, Jesus Christ, was the ultimate model of submission and obedience in His relationship with the heavenly Father. He also set the heavenly standard for every shepherd entrusted with God's sheep when He willingly laid down His life for His sheep. Paul the apostle closely followed the Lord's pattern in his selfless devotion to God's will and his sacrificial service to God's people. He remained closely related to the churches he had founded as a "father in the faith," often at great personal cost to himself. The weight of their care was upon him daily.

But I have all, and abound: I am full, having received of Epaphroditus the things which were sent from you, an odour of a sweet smell, a sacrifice acceptable, wellpleasing to God (Philippians 4:18).

I robbed other churches, taking wages of them, to do you service (2 Corinthians 11:8).

Apostolic People

It is important that I define what I mean by "apostolic people," because many will want to define the term incorrectly to wrongly enhance their own status or standing. An apostolic people is not a group of people who are all apostles (although an "apostolic company" may well match that definition).

An apostolic people is a group or body of people who have been "infected," inspired, and impelled by the Holy Spirit with the vision, work, and ministry of an apostle. They are happiest when they are directly or indirectly involved in the bold proclamation of the gospel and the establishment of churches and disciples "in Jerusalem, Judea, Samaria, and the uttermost parts of the world" (see Acts 1:8).

Apostolic people of every generation, location, and culture have these characteristics in common:

1. *Apostolic people have a broad global policy to reach the nations.*

   Although apostolic people are not necessarily pastored or led by an apostle, they have been touched by an apostolic dimension and vision. This dimension or impartation has altered their mind-set, transforming them into "sent out ones" as measured by their global view of God's purposes and by their "outward-looking" understanding, culture, and philosophy of ministry and Christian life (see Matt. 28:19; Ps. 2:7-9).

Apostolic people refuse to allow themselves to be limited, hindered, or bound by secular, cultural, socio-economic, or political obstacles or manmade boundaries. All limitations are broken down and overcome because, by God's design, their eyes look *beyond* the boundaries of their own geographical location. Their call is to spread the good news and proclaim the Kingdom of God to the ends of the earth personally or through their support of others.

They operate with an urgency because they are determined to finish God's stated goal of global evangelization. They are inherently unhappy and unsettled when they encounter "when we get to Heaven" theology, not because they do not believe in Heaven (because they do), but because they are not content to see God's glory cover the earth only in "the next generation." They long to see it come to pass now, in *this generation.*

2. *Apostolic people have a corporate and individual culture of prayer for the nations.*

All of God's people should pray God's heavenly Kingdom into the earth, into the hearts of individuals, and into the nations according to the model prayer Jesus gave us in Matthew 6:9-13.

Apostolic people in particular must have a corporate culture of prayer for the nations. Prayer is a lethal weapon that unlocks the doors to nations that have not been evangelized. Prayer is not confined to the geographical boundaries. It is an intercontinental ballistic missile of Heaven that can be sent from one geographical point to other countries and continents. When Daniel prayed, he caused a cosmic war!

The New Testament reveals that the early believers in the original apostolic church prayed for the boldness of apostles who were in relationship with their local fellowship. In our day, apostolic people pray together for the nations, for unreached people groups, for new regions, and for fellow workers at home and in distant locations.

3. *Apostolic people are faithful to send their money to support mission workers and mission work in foreign mission fields while being careful not to forget the poor and needy at home and in the greater Body of Christ.*

There is an inborn, Spirit-breathed desire in apostolic people to plant their material wealth and goods into ministry that is directly related to bringing the good news of Christ to the lost and to caring for the poor and fatherless. This is because such people are close to the Father-heart of God.

Moreover, brethren, we make known to you the grace of God bestowed on the churches of Macedonia: that in a great trial of affliction the abundance of their joy and their deep poverty abounded in the riches of their liberality. For I bear witness that according to their ability, yes, and beyond their ability, they were freely willing, imploring us with much urgency that we would receive the gift and the fellowship of the ministering to the saints. And not only as we had hoped, but they first gave themselves to the Lord, and then to us by the will of God (2 Corinthians 8:1-5 NKJV).

They desired only that we should remember the poor, the very thing which I also was eager to do (Galatians 2:10 NKJV).

For you know the grace of our Lord Jesus Christ, that though He was rich, yet for your sakes He became poor, that you through His poverty might become rich (2 Corinthians 8:9 NKJV).

4. *Apostolic people receive and honor the office of apostles, and they actively support and assist their ministry.*

Apostles tend to create an awareness among the saints about the importance of sending messengers of God's Kingdom to the ends of the earth. They are especially anointed by God to convey the "big picture" of God's greater purposes in the earth to local congregations as well as to help focus their resources on these works of God.

Apostles are also able to touch one of the "sacred cows" of the modern Church—the subject of money and giving. Many Christians who should know better become unreasonably paranoid or negative about money. Money is important only because it represents the life, time, energy, talents, and health that God has given to each of us. When we give money to God, we are giving our lives, time, energy, health, and talents.

Apostolic people are quick to give of themselves, their money, their prayers, and even their personal assistance to the purpose of world evangelism.

5. *Apostolic people are considered full partners in the work, ministry, and mission of apostles by God and by His apostles.*

According to the apostle Paul's letter to the church at Philippi, the believers in that city labored faithfully in partnership with him to support his preaching of the gospel.

I thank my God upon every remembrance of you, always in every prayer of mine for you all making request with joy, for your fellowship in the gospel from the first day until now...Even as it is meet for me to think this of you all, because I have you in my heart; inasmuch as both in my bonds, and in the defence and confirmation of the gospel, ye all are partakers of my grace (Philippians 1:3-5,7).

Another trait of God's apostolic people is that they are non-sectarian, supporting network relationships and the outreach projects to other people groups, regions, and nations with no desire to control.

Whensoever I take my journey into Spain, I will come to you: for I trust to see you in my journey, and to be brought on my way thitherward by you, if first I be somewhat filled with your company (Romans 15:24).

Yet I supposed it necessary to send to you Epaphroditus, my brother, and companion in labour, and fellowsoldier, but your messenger, and he that ministered to my wants (Philippians 2:25).

Apostolic people are motivated by a desire to see the Church succeed in the earth. This is simply a part of God's character anointing upon apostolic people, and it always inspires the free sharing of resources and even individual workers and leaders. Apostolic people tend to "adopt" apostles, apostolic works to other nations, and workers in those nations as their own. Apostolic passion and heart is for the *whole* Church, not just a few leaders.

The Operating Pattern of Apostolic Congregations

The "corporate culture" of the local church should go far beyond the activity of prayer. As an apostolic people, they should have a pattern of operating as *corporate body* of "sent ones" determined to fulfill the great commission of the Lord in Acts 1:8—to make disciples for Christ in Jerusalem, Judea, Samaria, and "to the end of the earth." Thus, the corporate culture of a local apostolic body or church will usually:

1. Pray corporately for the nations.
2. Have a corporate and a global policy for reaching out to the nations with the gospel of Jesus Christ.
3. Be a "sending church" that regularly sponsors and sends out long-term and short-term mission teams.
4. Be a giving church that joyfully invests themselves as well as their fervent prayers and money.
5. Be an "adopting church" that is quick to "adopt" people, groups, and gospel workers from other church bodies, ethnic groups, and nations as if they were their own.

How to "Receive Apostolic Ministry"

He that receiveth you receiveth me, and he that receiveth me receiveth him that sent me. He that receiveth a prophet in the name of a prophet shall receive a prophet's reward; and he that receiveth a righteous man in the name of a righteous man shall receive a righteous man's reward. And whosoever shall give to drink unto one of these little ones a cup of cold water only in the name of a disciple, verily I say unto you, he shall in no wise lose his reward (Matthew 10:40-42).

This teaching by Jesus clearly shows how God thinks about our treatment of others. Although we know God is "no respecter of persons" who shows no favoritism (Acts 10:34), we do know He has a very soft heart toward the brokenhearted, the weak, and the downtrodden. He is also very protective about the individuals who have chosen to sacrifice their freedom to pursue other interests in favor of laying down their lives and livelihoods to serve God's people.

Failure to receive apostles can leave us "desolate" or without apostolic impartation in the lives of our ministers and ministries. When we receive apostles, we are rewarded with the character anointing and impartation unique to the supernatural equipping gift of an apostle.

The apostolic dimension can be received by any local congregation, no matter where it is located. How can a local church tap into God's apostolic anointing and vision when it does not have an apostle resident in its congregation? The answer is found in the Lord and in prayer.

Ask the Lord for divine, God-ordained relationships with the apostolic ministry of His choice so you can begin to share visions, resources, and the blessings of obedience together. This is the nature of "divine networks" in the Kingdom. These *God-given* Kingdom connections should be accessed and brought into the life of the local church whenever the church leaders see the need for apostolic impartation into the local body. (However, I urge you to avoid artificial manmade relationships with so-called apostles who obviously pride themselves on their "title" and position. In this case, your fellowship has not joined with apostolic vision, but with fleshly folly.)

Three Types of Apostolic Relationships
With Local Churches

1. *Local Apostles.* Some churches are blessed with individuals in their congregations who have clearly been "called out" and set apart by the Holy Spirit for the work and office of apostle. In this case, the local church almost always has a corresponding call and grace from God to serve as an apostolic base from which the apostle will move to and fro in apostolic work and service. (Note: This does *not* necessarily mean this apostle is to pastor the host church, or even to occupy "first position" in the leadership of that church—although this is often the case.)

2. *Mobile or Itinerant Apostles.* Since the beginning of the Church recorded in the Book of Acts, there have been "traveling apostles" who were connected to one local church as a host or sending church, but who were also connected to networks of other local churches which they had either founded or for which they simply provided apostolic oversight or input as needed.

3. *Relational Apostles.* At this level, the local church will develop covenant relationships with several apostles who are accessed as the need arises.

Now we will go on to examine the many aspects of true apostolic ministry in the Church of Jesus Christ.

Endnote

1. I've chosen not to use the word *mentor*, although it is a term in common use today. It is derived from non-biblical Greek mythology. Mentor was the name of a friend of Odysseus; Mentor was entrusted with the

education of Odysseus' son during his wanderings allegedly chronicled in Homer's epic poem, *The Odyssey*. In any case, other words such as *teacher*, *instructor*, *father*, and *guide* are well suited to the task.

Chapter 6

The Ministry of an Apostle

The ministry of the apostle has been misunderstood by people in the Church for centuries. Many church leaders acted on their doubts by carefully relegating the apostle to the "ancient history" of the Book of Acts and the first century Church; God, however, has never been confused or double-minded about the gift He gave to the Church, the gift called the apostle.

As the apostle Paul explained to the Ephesians, Jesus Christ Himself gave the five equipping gifts or ascension gifts to the Church for two main purposes: to perfect the saints and to equip the saints for the work of the ministry.

Since the Church is obviously not perfect yet and since it is not fully equipped or engaged in the work of the ministry (most of this work is being done by "professional clergy" instead of by the believers as a whole), the Church *needs* the vital ministry of the apostle today.

Many "cessationists" (those who believe that the offices of apostle and prophet ceased or died away with the original disciples of the Lamb and Paul) try to take away these two vital gifts while clinging to the three they feel still exist—all without any firm support from the Bible. Yet we cannot cling to the offices of evangelist, pastor, and teacher without also embracing the two remaining gifts with them to comprise the whole of the Lord's leadership package: the apostle and the prophet. By their actions, leaders who deny the existence of apostles today are depriving their churches of a number of absolutely vital services provided by the thoroughly biblical office of the apostle.

1. The Apostle: Foundational Gift for the New Testament Church

According to the apostle Paul, the Church was and is built upon the foundation of the apostles and prophets.

> *Now therefore ye* [Gentiles or non-Jews] *are no more strangers and foreigners, but fellowcitizens with the saints, and of the household of God; and are built upon the foundation of the apostles and prophets, Jesus Christ himself being the chief corner stone; in whom all the building fitly framed together groweth unto an holy temple in the Lord: in whom ye also are builded together for an habitation of God through the Spirit* (Ephesians 2:19-22).

The Greek word translated as "foundation" in this passage is *themelios*, meaning "something put down, i.e. a substruction (of a building, etc.). Literally or figuratively, it is derived from a root word that refers to the placement of something 'in a passive or horizontal posture.' "[1]

This is a picture of the first of the five *doma* gifts of God described in the Book of Ephesians where Paul wrote,

56

"Wherefore he saith, When he ascended up on high, he led captivity captive, and gave *gifts* [*doma*] unto men" (Eph. 4:8); and also:

> *And he gave some, apostles; and some, prophets; and some, evangelists; and some, pastors and teachers; for the perfecting of the saints, for the work of the ministry, for the edifying of the body of Christ: till we all come in the unity of the faith, and of the knowledge of the Son of God, unto a perfect man...* (Ephesians 4:11-13).

The apostle is not simply one who "receives" a *charis* gift such as prophecy or the discernment of spirits. He *is* literally *the gift* given to the Body of Christ; he is one who lays down his life in sacrificial, pioneering ministry as a foundation stone for his sheep just as the Great Shepherd did before him. (An alternative translation of the original Greek may well read, "...He gave gift-people"—*doma anthropos*.)

This statement by Paul is to be understood on two levels, as are most New Testament teachings. First it applied to the New Testament Church in a historical sense. The coming of Jesus Christ the Chief Cornerstone was predicted ahead of time by the prophets of old (such as Isaiah and Jeremiah) and was confirmed by prophets contemporary to His own time (John the Baptist, Anna, and Simeon). The Church was "launched" upon the inspired preaching of Peter the apostle on the Day of Pentecost, and it was carried forward on the ministries, testimony, and teachings of the apostles of the Lamb. However, the foundational work of apostles and prophets *did not stop there*!

Although not all apostles found churches, many do. Apostles are pioneers, "sent ones" with a unique anointing to break new ground and establish the work of God in new territories. The New Testament pattern often included the work of an evangelist as well, who would preach the gospel of Christ and win converts. Then he would contact the home church, which in turn would "send" or dispatch apostles and prophets to confirm and establish the church on firm foundations while the evangelist would move on to new areas.

2. The Apostle: Apt to Teach, Apt to Duplicate His Gift and Raise Up Disciples

Whereunto I am appointed a preacher, and an apostle, and a teacher of the Gentiles (2 Timothy 1:11).

True apostles are balanced between the Word of God and the need for the Spirit and the supernatural. As with all the five ascension gifts or "elders," the apostle must be "apt to teach" (2 Tim. 2:24). This is especially important since the apostle is uniquely equipped and anointed to raise up other ministry gifts. (Some respected leaders teach that apostles should operate in at least three of the five ascension gift ministries instead of just one.)

Teaching is especially important where apostles establish new works of God in regions where knowledge of God and His Word is nonexistent. This was demonstrated in Paul's pattern of establishing churches in Asia, where he often spent years teaching new believers in synagogues, school buildings, and other locations. Only when a firm foundation in the Word was established and new ministry gifts raised up or assigned from elsewhere would he consider moving on to new works.

3. The Apostle: Deeply Involved in and Responsible for Church Discipline

But I will come to you shortly, if the Lord will, and will know, not the speech of them which are puffed up, but the power. For the kingdom of God is not in word, but in power. What will ye? shall I come unto you with a rod, or in love, and in the spirit of meekness? (1 Corinthians 4:19-21).

Now I beseech you, brethren, mark them which cause divisions and offences contrary to the doctrine which ye have learned; and avoid them (Romans 16:17).

The disciplining and correcting of saints is part of an apostle's work, particularly in those churches founded by the respective apostle. In other cases, it is the apostle who is called in to mediate and decide interchurch differences and to speak apostolicly into the life, government, and direction of the church in cooperation with the pastor of the flock. The apostle is also called in to handle problems connected with ethical, moral, or doctrinal breaches by pastors or local church leadership.

Paul specifically addressed the problem of open fornication and incest in the church at Corinth and pronounced the appropriate discipline.

It is reported commonly that there is fornication among you, and such fornication as is not so much as named among the Gentiles, that one should have his father's wife. And ye are puffed up, and have not rather mourned, that he that hath done this deed might be taken away from among you. For I verily, as absent in body, but present in spirit, have judged already, as though I were present, concerning him that hath so done this deed, in the name of our Lord Jesus Christ, when ye are gathered together, and my spirit, with the power of our Lord Jesus Christ, to deliver such an one unto Satan for the destruction of the flesh, that the spirit may be saved in the day of the Lord Jesus (1 Corinthians 5:1-5).

The apostle again addressed the church in his second letter to Corinth urging the church to forgive the offending brother after he complied with the prescribed church discipline (see 2 Cor. 2:6-11).

4. The Apostle's Fatherlike Care for the Churches

Beside those things that are without, that which cometh upon me daily, the care of all the churches (2 Corinthians 11:28).

At the core of his being, the apostle is a pastor's pastor with a deep and abiding concern for the spiritual order and welfare of the churches and church leaders with whom he is associated. The weight of this concern never leaves him, just as a father's love and concern for his children never leave his heart or mind.

5. The True Apostle Brings Wisdom to All of His Work

According to the grace of God which is given unto me, as a wise masterbuilder, I have laid the foundation, and another buildeth thereon. But let every man take heed how he buildeth thereupon (1 Corinthians 3:10).

Wisdom hath builded her house, she hath hewn out her seven pillars (Proverbs 9:1).

Since the apostle is the master builder of the five ascension gifts, the spirit of wisdom is a very important and essential part of the apostle's "tool" kit. Chapters 8 and 9 of the Book of Proverbs speak of one who builds a house. In fact, the builder of the house is the very embodiment of Wisdom, a picture of the indwelling Spirit of God working within His New Testament master builders, the apostles.

6. The Apostle: A Guardian of Order and Proper Relationships

In any family, and especially in the family of God and the Body of Christ, there exists a vital need for order, structure, organization, and universal rules of conduct for smooth functioning. The apostolic office at times may require the apostle to function as lawmaker, law enforcement officer, mediator, and judge. This is why this office can only be fulfilled supernaturally by the gift and grace of God.

*And if any man hunger, let him eat at home; that ye come not together unto condemnation. And **the rest will I set in order when I come*** (1 Corinthians 11:34).

*But as God hath distributed to every man, as the Lord hath called every one, so let him walk. And **so ordain I in all churches*** (1 Corinthians 7:17).

*Now concerning the collection for the saints, **as I have given order to the churches** of Galatia, even so do ye. Upon the first day of the week let every one of you lay by him in store, as God hath prospered him, that there be no gatherings when I come* (1 Corinthians 16:1-2).

*And **if any man obey not our word** by this epistle, note that man, and have no company with him, that he may be ashamed* (2 Thessalonians 3:14).

*For though I be absent in the flesh, **yet am I with you in the spirit, joying and beholding your order**, and the stedfastness of your faith in Christ* (Colossians 2:5).

7. The Apostle Strengthens the Churches

And when they had preached the gospel to that city, and had taught many, they returned again to Lystra, and to Iconium, and Antioch, confirming the souls of the disciples, and exhorting them to continue in the faith, and that we must through much tribulation enter into the kingdom of God (Acts 14:21-22).

8. The Apostle Appoints Elders (Ministers) in the Churches

And when they had ordained them elders in every church, and had prayed with fasting, they commended them to the Lord, on whom they believed (Acts 14:23).

[Paul to Timothy] *Neglect not the gift that is in thee, which was given thee by prophecy, with the laying on of the hands of the presbytery* (1 Timothy 4:14).

The apostles appointed and ordained ministers in the churches they established after prayer with fasting and by the laying on of hands.

9. Apostles Excel in the Direction and Confirmation of Saints in Their Call and Ministry in the Body

And he gave some, apostles; and some, prophets; and some, evangelists; and some, pastors and teachers; for the perfecting of the saints, for the work of the ministry, for the edifying of the body of Christ (Ephesians 4:11-12).

Even as the great Apostle was the first to confirm and ordain the call of God on the lives of apostles and the other four *doma* or ascension leadership gifts, true apostles today should exhibit a special ability to discern and activate the gifts in believers' lives and to train and ordain those believers in their ministry.

Understanding Apostleship

There are sometimes noticeable differences in the various administrations of different apostolic anointings. The key to understanding apostleship is to *know to whom an apostle is sent*. Peter was sent to the Jews, although he also was chosen by God to open the door of salvation to the Gentiles in the house of Cornelius (see Acts 10). The remaining eleven "apostles of the Lamb" were also sent to the Jews. Paul the apostle, on the other hand, was sent to the Gentiles.

Some apostles were sent to specific nations or regions, and others were primarily identified with specific cities and local churches. We will quickly step into error if we expect all apostles to be exactly alike or to have the same measure of grace or gift of Christ. *By God's design*, the diversity of apostles seen in the New Testament did not function in the same dimension of anointing. One comparative glance between Peter and Paul is enough to solidly establish this point. It appears that the Lord used this diversity to balance the strengths and weaknesses of the men He had called as leaders.

The Importance of Understanding Your Measure

According to the grace of God which is given unto me, as a wise masterbuilder, I have laid the foundation, and another buildeth thereon. But let every man take heed how he buildeth thereupon (1 Corinthians 3:10).

One of the most important pieces of advice a Christian can receive is this counsel: "Operate within your grace." This is especially true for apostles and the other ascension leadership gifts in the Church (prophets, evangelists, pastors, and teachers). This may or may not have anything to do with your natural abilities or learned skills or background.

Paul, the "seminary-trained" intellectual Pharisee-rabbi with an impeccable Jewish pedigree, seemed perfectly suited to minister to the Jews. God, however, sent him to convert Gentiles in pagan lands.

Peter, the hot-tempered career fisherman from lowly Galilee (who was probably poorly educated compared to the average Jewish man of his day), seemed better suited to reach Gentiles. Yet by God's grace, his greatest effectiveness came on the Day of Pentecost when he led thousands to Christ with one inspired sermon and witnessed the literal birth of the Church at Jerusalem in one day.

James, the brother of Jesus, was best suited as the "senior elder" and pastor of the Jerusalem congregation. We don't hear of him traveling to other churches or visiting Gentile congregations. He also was gifted to boldly stand for Christ against the Jewish and Roman power structures in Jerusalem.

John, "the apostle whom Jesus loved," was best known during Jesus' ministry as the disciple who loved to be near Jesus all the time. It was John who leaned against Jesus' chest during the last supper. He wasn't known or recognized for great spirituality, outspokenness, or strength and endurance. Yet John, alone of all the disciples, evidently died a natural death in exile for Christ's gospel. It was John who saw the great Revelation of Christ on the Isle of Patmos and unveiled the eternal panorama of God's great plan of redemption and total victory over the enemy and death itself.

Each of these ordinary men had an extraordinary measure of grace from God, and each prospered as long as they remained within the boundaries of their unique calling and God-ordained ministry. Peter came closest to wandering off course when he failed to separate his Jewish background and his friends from his calling to honor the vision of God about the acceptance of the Gentiles into God's family (in a manner strikingly similar to his denial of Christ in the courtyard of the high priest years before). Paul had to openly rebuke him for giving in to the peer pressure of his legalistic Jewish friends.

Peter returned to his calling from Jesus to "feed My sheep" and courageously died on a cross for His Lord. Church history claims that Peter felt unworthy to die as His Master had died, so he requested that his executioners crucify him upside down on the cross, and his final request was granted.

He returned to his area of grace and finished his course in glory and honor.

Paul the apostle knew about the "measure of grace" and applied this knowledge specifically to describe the limits of his apostolic authority in his second letter to the church at Corinth:

> *For we dare not make ourselves of the number, or compare ourselves with some that commend themselves: but they measuring themselves by themselves, and comparing themselves among themselves, are not wise. But we will not boast of things **without our measure**, but according to **the measure of the rule which God hath distributed to us**, a measure to reach even unto you. For we stretch not ourselves **beyond our measure**, as though we reached not unto you: for we are come as far as to you also in preaching the gospel of Christ* (2 Corinthians 10:12-14).

The limits or boundaries of your God-given grace are directly connected to your personal assignment and purpose in the Lord. What is your purpose in life? What is the reason for your birth? Why did God give you breath and life? You know by the Spirit dwelling in your inner man that there are certain things you must do with your life.

1. Your grace from God will empower you to finish your divine assignment successfully.
2. Paul was careful to lay the foundations of his ministry as a master builder in accordance with the grace and empowerment given to him. You must be careful to do the same.
3. Remember: You can only deposit that which has been deposited into you. If you deposit a certain amount of money into the bank, you cannot withdraw a single

penny more than you deposited without incurring an overdraft penalty. Many young ministers have tried to operate on "borrowed anointing and experience" that they didn't have and experienced great failure in their lives. You cannot impart what has not been given to you. Minister out of your abundance in Christ. Peter told the beggar at the Gate beautiful in Jerusalem, "…Silver and gold have I none; but **such as I have give I thee**: In the name of Jesus Christ of Nazareth rise up and walk" (Acts 3:6). The best thing we can ever give is the living Christ Jesus who dwells within us.

4. It is vital for each of us to "think soberly" about our calling and purpose in Christ. Then we must be careful to operate within that measure of grace— neither under nor above our proper measure. Paul wrote to the Church at Rome:

    For I say, through the grace given unto me, to every man that is among you, not to think of himself more highly than he ought to think; but to think soberly, according as God hath dealt to every man the measure of faith. For as we have many members in one body, and all members have not the same office: so we, being many, are one body in Christ, and every one members one of another. Having then gifts differing according to the grace that is given to us, whether prophecy, let us prophesy according to the proportion of faith (Romans 12:3-6).

In God's divine economy, He gives gifts to believers differently. Your grace is your equipment. Grace is given in accordance to the will of the Holy Spirit. Paul told the Ephesians, "But unto every one of us *is given grace* according to the measure of the gift of Christ" (Eph. 4:7). First God gave His Son as the greatest gift of all, then Jesus the Son gave leadership gifts to the Church to continue His work on earth and to help prepare His Bride. Paul knew the source of ministry gift was God's grace:

> *Whereof I was made a minister,* ***according to the gift of the grace of God*** *given unto me by the effectual working of His power. Unto me, who am less than the least of all saints, is* ***this grace given****, that I should preach among the Gentiles the unsearchable riches of Christ* (Ephesians 3:7-8).

Your grace is your boundary stone. When you operate outside the measure of your grace, you operate in weakness and frustration. The most important area of an apostle's ministry requiring God's grace is in his role as a spiritual father to sons and daughters of the King.

Endnote

1. James Strong, *Strong's Exhaustive Concordance of the Bible* (Peabody, MA: Hendrickson Publishers, n.d.), **foundation** (#G2310, G5087).

Chapter 7

The Apostle as Spiritual Father

God does not communicate in a vacuum. He always speaks into the context of our daily lives and current experiences, expressing spiritual truth and principles in ways that can be practiced and lived. In Scripture, God paints pictures of diverse leadership gifts that He placed in the Church to illustrate His desired leadership structure in ways that we can relate to and embrace in our particular cultural context.

The office and function of the apostle, "the father-like one," is one of God's most unique revelations of His own leadership anointing and nature.[1] The Scriptures continually help us learn about the character of God through historic and prophetic "snapshots" of His relationship with mankind, and the fatherhood of God is one of the most pervasive of all biblical images of His divine nature.

This central aspect of God's relationship with us is most deeply revealed and cultivated within the dynamics of *family relationships*. Whether we look at the intimate portraits of God the Father's relationship with Jesus the Son in the New Testament, or at the intimate dealings of God with Moses, Abraham, David, and the prophets, we see our Lord dealing with men, communicating and interacting *in the chosen role of Father* to His beloved children.

This fact is beyond refutation or argument: Our God is a loving Father who faithfully loves, cares for, provides for, and disciplines His children. It is in this eternal paternal role that God expresses His nature through the office, function, and anointing of the apostle as father. The writer of the Book of Hebrews tells us:

For every house is builded by some man; but he that built all things is God. And Moses verily was faithful in all his [God's] *house, as a servant, for a testimony of those things which were to be spoken after; but Christ as a son over his own house; whose house are we, if we hold fast the confidence and the rejoicing of the hope firm unto the end* (Hebrews 3:4-6).

Jesus Christ lives and ministers in the family as our Elder Brother solely because the chief aim of His sacrificial death was to win the right for all true believers to become *the children of God*: "But as many as received him [Jesus], to them gave he power to become the sons of God, even to them that believe on his name" (John 1:12). Isaiah the prophet declared, "But now, O Lord, *thou art our father*; we are the clay, and thou our potter; and we all are the work of thy hand" (Is. 64:8). This revelation of His fatherhood is at the heart of God's supernatural agenda for this generation.

70

The Restoration of Fathers

Even as God is raising up apostles or "father-like ones" in the Church today, there is a strategic attack from the pit of hell aimed at destroying the nucleus of the family in the societies of the world and in the Church.

One of the most visible areas of concern is the growing problem of parents who abdicate their responsibility toward their children. The runaway divorce epidemic sweeping through the nations is leaving behind millions of devastated children who are forced to grow up in single-parent homes without the steadying influence of both birth parents. The ordeal endured by these innocent victims negatively conditions their thinking, perceptions, and values for parental roles, personal identity, and proper function in the family unit.

Children who grow up in an environment of broken family relationships are placed at a disadvantage because they do not relate to their fathers and mothers as positive role models in the family. Paul noted in First Corinthians 15 that the first Adam and Jesus Christ the "second Adam" represent parallel truths related to the fall and redemption of mankind, then added, "Howbeit that was not first which is spiritual, but that which is natural [Adam]; and afterward that which is spiritual [Christ]" (verse 46).

The natural often signals a parallel reality in the spiritual. It is likely that the lack of fathers as role models in the family is an indication of the spiritual climate in the Church, where there is a lack of fathering leadership. Just as fathers in the natural have abdicated their fathering responsibilities, so too have "fathers" in the family of God denied the Church a wealth of nurturing leadership.

The Church is God's alternative society in the world. In God's family, relationships are not governed or dictated by divisions of age, sex, culture, or status. Instead, the Church models a corporate family life that is based on biblical principles and values. Our relationship to authority is a crucial foundation—for better or for worse—of family life and of every local church and the Church worldwide.

The Generation That Curses Its Fathers

According to Proverbs 30:11, "There is a generation that curseth their father, and doth not bless their mother." This biblical description of the core weakness of an entire generation points to attitudes and behavior that are devoid of love and communication. A generation that speaks evil of its fathers is a generation that experiences definite alienation. The Hebrew word translated as "curse" means "bringing into contempt, to despise or to make light."[2] Therefore, just as children in the natural speak evil against their fathers due to wrong models of fathering, so too there is a level of discontentment and verbal frustration with leaders in the Church who do not fulfill their fathering role.

The children of a father-cursing generation will clamor to "uncover" their father's weakness and expose their father's failures. The Bible describes the differing responses of Noah's sons to their father's nakedness and weakness in Genesis 9:20-28. Ham "uncovered" or wrongfully exposed and proclaimed his father's nakedness by instinctively reporting to his brothers that their father was lying naked in his tent.

Shem and Japheth, on the other hand, carefully avoided collaborating with Ham's attempts to expose their father. They laid a garment over their shoulders and entered their father's tent backwards to cover his nakedness. That way they avoided seeing their father's weakness or exposing it further. It is a sad reality that many spiritual children delight in ridicule, and are eager to publicly discredit their spiritual fathers and leaders.

Isaiah the prophet dealt with the other side of the problem when he issued a strong indictment against fathers who fail to rear or properly raise their sons and daughters (see Is. 23:4). The ability to procreate is not the primary qualifying factor in defining a man as a father. Rather, it is the difficult lifelong process of "rearing" children that quickly separates the real men from the immature boys. To "rear" connotes a continuous process of teaching, tutoring, and modeling. It is an intensive process in which a father bonds with his child and imprints character and a sense of identity within his offspring.

This paternal bond is crucial to the development of a child's inner sense of security and self-worth, and it is a major determinant of a child's social, mental, emotional, and spiritual development. This vital aspect of fathering "leadership" within the Church is also an indicator of the sincerity and commitment of fathers to their children. In other words, as the individual fathers have healthy relationships with their children, so will the fathers in the church have healthy relationships with the people of God.

Fathers within the Body of Christ need to take time to listen and understand their sons and daughters. They should also do whatever it takes to guide them into maturity within the context of the local church family under God's love and authority.

Despite the scenario of unending conflict in our society where children "naturally" despise their fathers and where fathers "naturally" abdicate their responsibilities as men, husbands, and fathers, God has a different plan. He is His own eternal standard of fatherhood in perfection. According to that standard, He intends to restore the precious relationships between fathers and children through the finished work of His Son, Jesus Christ.

Through God's intervention, the broken relationships between fathers and their estranged sons and daughters can be restored. Every chasm of isolation, bitterness, and simmering hostility can be bridged. Every relationship of strife can be transformed into a relationship of cooperation, mutual trust, and love.

We serve a miracle-working God, and He has focused all the resources of Heaven on healing the breached relationship between fathers and children. His final promise of the Old Covenant must be fulfilled as He declared in the last verse of the last book of the Old Testament:

> *And he* [Elijah, symbolizing Jesus the Messiah] *shall turn the heart of the fathers to the children, and the heart of the children to their fathers, lest I come and smite the earth with a curse* (Malachi 4:6).

God wants to change the hearts of both fathers and children. No longer must blame be shifted and conflict tolerated. In their place, God wants to see a reciprocal relationship spring up from changed hearts. This is what is needed to infuse life into the fractured relationship between fathers and children.

Examples of Spiritual Fathers

1. *David* called *Saul* "father" although the jealous king had done little to deserve it.

   > *Moreover, my father, see! Yes, see that corner of your robe in my hand! For in that I cut off the corner of your robe, and did not kill you, know and see that there is neither evil nor rebellion in my hand, and I have not sinned against you. Yet you hunt my life to take it* (1 Samuel 24:11 NKJV).

2. *Elisha* called *Elijah* "father" in the Book of Second Kings.

And Elisha saw it, and he cried out, "My father, my father, the chariot of Israel and its horsemen!" So he saw him no more. And he took hold of his own clothes and tore them into two pieces (2 Kings 2:12 NKJV).

3. The *prodigal son* who selfishly took his inheritance and wasted it in sin rediscovered a *loving father* who was waiting with his arms and heart opened wide in forgiveness, welcome, and joy. This is a beautiful picture of the unconditional love of our heavenly Father, of a godly earthly father, and of a true spiritual father in the Church (see Luke 15:11-32).

4. *Timothy* faithfully served Paul, and *Paul* called Timothy his son (see 1 Cor. 4:17).

The Eternal Responsibilities of Fathers

1. *Love.* In the natural, some fathers are good providers but do not know how to express their love to their children. This causes rejection and a lack of communication between children and parents. Many people who grew up in this environment carry this problem into their relationship with God when they get saved. However, God's Word reminds us to remember that God loves us unconditionally.

2. *Protection.* Children need to feel protected. If anyone threatens my child, I would stand up to protect him—no matter how big the person is. The Holy Spirit spoke to me about this once and said, "How much more your Father in Heaven wants to do for you." Our Father God wants to stand up against every enemy that comes up against us, because we are His blood-bought children. God wants to protect us from every evil, harm, and danger.

3. *Reproduction.* True spiritual fathers birth movements, ministries, and vision, and where there are apostles, there should always be an element of progress in evidence. Fathers want their sons to increase in influence and in the ministry, exceeding the standards set by their fathers. Fathers take joy in watching their sons surpass their own accomplishments and victories. Every victory and accomplishment creates foundations in their sons' lives that will break limitations.

4. *Discipleship and training.* True spiritual fathers are able to rightly discern the times and to perceive the seasons that the Church is about to enter. Therefore, they have an anointing to train leaders who are able to deal with the conflicts involved in ministry in their season. Spiritual fathers possess a wealth of acquired wisdom and insight that help them train existing leaders and leaders-to-be to be more effective in ministry. Fathers, in their role as guides and instructors, bring the course adjustments or corrections needed to help their spiritual sons move beyond their limitations safely.

5. *Government.* Fathers fulfill a governmental role in the family, and apostles, as spiritual fathers, fulfill a key government role in the family of God. Apostles, as spiritual fathers exercising oversight among the churches and various ministry gifts, bring a dimension of governmental anointing into the life of the family of God. They work closely with local pastors, elders, and congregations to bring direction, guidance, and the efficient matching of callings, gifts, and abilities with ministry needs, personal needs, and daily family needs of the larger Body of Christ.

6. *Discipline.* Every family needs law and order to truly flourish, and for this reason Scripture places fathers in an important position. Not only are they to function as the

head of the home, but fathers also are personally responsible for training and administering discipline to their children when necessary. This governmental function helps to establish order in a home. No human being is born into a family automatically knowing how the family is structured and governed. However, parents use instruction and discipline to define and demonstrate for their children the meaning and importance of morality, social values, and spiritual beliefs.

And ye have forgotten the exhortation which speaketh unto you as unto children, My son, despise not thou the chastening of the Lord, nor faint when thou art rebuked of him: for whom the Lord loveth he chasteneth, and scourgeth every son whom he receiveth. If ye endure chastening, God dealeth with you as with sons; for what son is he whom the father chasteneth not? But if ye be without chastisement, whereof all are partakers, then are ye bastards, and not sons. Furthermore we have had fathers of our flesh which corrected us, and we gave them reverence: shall we not much rather be in subjection unto the Father of spirits, and live? For they verily for a few days chastened us after their own pleasure; but he for our profit, that we might be partakers of his holiness. Now no chastening for the present seemeth to be joyous, but grievous: nevertheless afterward it yieldeth the peaceable fruit of righteousness unto them which are exercised thereby (Hebrews 12:5-11).

The refusal to discipline a child is *not* an expression of love; rather, it is an expression of neglect and shame. Any father who allows his son to do what he pleases shows that he regards that son as no better than an illegitimate child to whom he feels neither love nor responsibility.

The Restoration of the Fathering Ministry

*And I will clothe him with thy robe, and strengthen him
with thy girdle, and I will commit thy government into
his hand: and he shall be a father to the inhabitants of
Jerusalem, and to the house of Judah. And the key of
the house of David will I lay upon his shoulder; so he
shall open, and none shall shut; and he shall shut, and
none shall open. And I will fasten him as a nail in a
sure place; and he shall be for a glorious throne to his
father's house* (Isaiah 22:21-23).

Isaiah the prophet was prophesying the Lord's intention to
remove Shebna, who was an evil "father" or steward over
David's house. Since Shebna had neglected his duties, God
was going to replace him with Eliakim, a man who would
restore the proper father-like care God intends for every
godly leader to exhibit and demonstrate in service and leadership. The nature of the work of the father is *to build according to the design of God.* A father builds up his heritage, his
offspring, by covering, governing, and strengthening them in
the Lord.

1. *Covering (or clothing).* Fathers cover and protect
   their children. This protective covering does not
   shield children so much that it makes them dependent on their fathers. Instead, it equips the children to
   stand and wage war with confidence. Fathers also
   wrap or clothe their children in their mantle of
   anointing.
2. *Governing.* Fathers rule or rightly order their home
   according to the righteous standards of God (not
   their own fleshly standards), wielding the delegated
   authority of God.

3. *Strengthening*. Fathers strengthen their children so they will be strong and courageous, to be a cure (instead of a cause of disease), to help, to repair and fortify, to conquer, and to confirm and establish. This speaks of reformation. God did not place the Church in man's (the male) hand for men to determine the design and pattern for the family of God. The Lord will supply each man a pattern and blueprint for the home, just as He gave Noah a pattern for the ark and Moses and David the "blueprints" for the dwelling place of God.

The Role of a Father

1. *Attitude of Children*
   A. Learn from the natural—a son should always know that the inheritance he has come into is his *because of his father*. He should honor his father for this.
   B. No matter how gifted, talented, charismatic, or educated a son may be, he must not forget the respect and authority that come with the position of being a father. As soon as the father enters into his son's presence, the son will respect the authority of his father, even though the son may be more influential or gifted than his father in later years. Sons may try to run a house, but the father authority is the only authority recognized by the rest of the family. This is proper spiritual authority from which we can learn in the natural.
   C. One of the first commandments with promise is to honor our mothers and fathers. The Bible does not say we should honor them "if they are good" and dishonor them "if they are irresponsible."
      • One of Noah's sons failed to honor his father when he openly uncovered his sin in Genesis

9:22. His two others sons preserved their father's honor by covering his sin. *Love always covers.*

- David's son, Absalom, rebelled against his father and died in rebellion (see 2 Sam. 17–18). The rebellious live in a dry and wicked land.
- Saul was a back-slidden "pastor" attending the services of a witch, but still David respectfully called him the Lord's anointed.
- We should also be careful about the way we deal with fathers. We have a right, if we feel manipulated and disagree, to leave our fathers agreeably. We should not hurt him or the rest of the family through un-Christlike behavior and conduct. We should never seek to hurt the members of the Body of Christ.

2. *The Attitude of Sons During Discipline*

And, ye fathers, provoke not your children to wrath: but bring them up in the nurture and admonition of the Lord (Ephesians 6:4).

Children need to understand that correction is not necessarily rejection. The same is true for the Church family. When discipline is administered in ministries or local churches, in most cases the people who were disciplined attempt to leave. They may not realize it, but the Bible calls them bastards and illegitimate sons born out of wedlock (see Heb. 12:7-8). There are many "bastards" in the Church today who have fled their fathers' authority. When disciplined, they quickly run to other ministries who have become little more than orphanages and day care centers for the immature and uncorrected. They are refuge centers with foster parents, and at worst are reformatories and institutes for "juvenile delinquents."

If we perceive ourselves to be a David under a cruel and abusive Saul who is chasing us with javelins to destroy us, we must understand that it is God who puts us in these circumstances to put iron into our character. The things we face under Saul's unfair rule have to do with our destiny. We must understand that this time of survival will only last until the time appointed by the Father.

We can learn much from David's attitude toward a father. In conflict David had the opportunity to destroy Saul, but did not abuse his authority or rush his own call to the throne by usurping the throne of another. He understood that he was dealing with a man whom God had placed above him and that *God should deal with him.*

3. *Problem Periods in Fathering*

There are different stages of development in children. Sixteen-year-olds always think they know more than Dad. They think that they are ready for adult responsibilities and privileges, so it shouldn't be surprising that a few problems arise at this stage.

A. Responsibility (or authority) without accountability always causes problems.

B. Some fathers are too slow in their judgment or discernment of the growth and progression of their children. In other words, to these fathers, their sons will always be their little boys and their daughters will always be their little girls. This can be very unhealthy for the children.

C. If sons are not released, *they will leave home.*

D. It should be understood that some sons will serve their fathers for all their lives, while others will have to leave to raise up their own families and children. During this period a smooth transition should be enforced. If a son leaves the house, he should be encouraged with the help of the father and other family members to build a home. If a son is to take over his father's house, again it should be over a transitional period of several years, with the father releasing more and more authority and responsibility with accountability. The time frame can be determined together. This way the whole house experiences the blessings of change.

4. *Attitudes of Fathers*
   A. Fathers are never intimidated by sons. Fathers want the best for their sons.
   B. Brothers are afraid of brothers. The "elder brother syndrome" surfaces when the elder brother is unhappy when the younger one is blessed and welcomed by the father. The heart of a father is to develop the potential within all his children (see Luke 15).
   C. A father wants to see his children outgrow him.
   D. A father's heart is to equip and develop the gifts, passion, and intellect of his children.
   E. Fathers want to see their children outgrow their ministries and become more successful than themselves.

5. *Fathers Leave a Legacy*

Expect your ministry to go beyond your years. Extend your ministry to the future generation; envision it as a ministry beyond the grave. This is a legacy that you, as a father, must leave for your sons. Fathers make provisions for their children long after they have left this earth. Second Corinthians 12:14 teaches that "children ought not to lay up for the parents, but the parents for the children." As physical and spiritual parents, it is our responsibility to ensure that our children have the necessary advantages in life by providing for their security even after we have died.

Abraham, the father of our faith, ensured that he left a legacy behind for his children. The covenant between God and Abraham is detailed in Genesis 12:

And I will make of thee a great nation, and I will bless thee, and make thy name great; and thou shalt be a blessing: and I will bless them that bless thee, and curse him that curseth thee: and in thee shall all families of the earth be blessed (Genesis 12:2-3).

God's call to Abraham contained three aspects. Those aspects were the *reality of descendants*, a *covenant relationship*, and the *inheritance of the territory*. Abraham's quest for nationhood is the history of his children, and he leaves them with that legacy. Jacob also gave an inheritance to his twelve sons.

The Book of Proverbs says, "House and riches are the inheritance of fathers" (Prov. 19:14a). Fathers in the Church need to develop this mentality of knowing that their ministry, work, and life influence not just their generation, but also generations to come. Therefore, fathers are to leave ministries and resources and impart vision to their sons.

The heart and desire of every father is to leave a legacy for his children. I am a father with two children. My desire is that they have more than I had as a child, that they have a better education and future, and that they grow up in a better environment. So it is with the heart of the apostle, the father-like one.

Endnotes

1. Some may raise their eyebrows when they read this statement, but it is not as far out there as it may appear. It is generally understood that the five *doma* gifts given to the Church by Jesus and listed by Paul in Ephesians 4 each represent a portion of Christ, the Anointed One,

who was Himself the *fullness* of the Godhead bodily. Inasmuch as the apostle reflects even a fraction of the nature and leadership anointing of Jesus Christ in the earth, then the apostle is genuinely a reflection, ilustration, and revelation of God's leadership anointing and nature in part.

2. James Strong, *Strong's Exhaustive Concordance of the Bible* (Peabody, MA: Hendrickson Publishers, n.d.), **curse** (*qalal*, #H7043).

Chapter 8

The Marks of an Apostle

Truly the signs of an apostle were wrought among you in all patience, in signs, and wonders, and mighty deeds (2 Corinthians 12:12).

If you ask liberal theologians and church leaders, they will tell you that one of the most aggravating aspects of the Greek words associated with the miracles in the New Testament is that they imply acts and events that clearly *violate* the laws of nature. This is not only true of our modern understanding, but also applied to the understanding of the people of the New Testament era.

The only way to "remove" miracles from the New Testament is to totally tear down the validity of Christ's ministry and the ministry of the apostles after the Lord's resurrection. The problem is that their ministries were so "supernatural."

The truth is that this is no problem at all. It is evidence of the presence of a supernatural God working through people in supernatural power. All this was complicated by a dichotomy or division of worldviews between the Jews who were called "a people of signs" and the Greeks who were supposedly predominately "rational." (The rationalists only believed what could be reasoned and verified by external proofs.)

The same dichotomy exists today! The western world (including all of Europe and North America) views signs, wonders, and miracles with skepticism. This is not the case in South America, Asia, or with the nations of Africa. In these places, the people receive the supernatural with childlike faith.

As a citizen of South Africa, and having lived and ministered in a culture where more people come into the Kingdom of God through signs and wonders than any other way, I can clearly see and understand the need for signs and wonders to *increase* in the life of the Church worldwide!

Rational argument is good as far as it goes, but as many a missionary has quickly discovered in Africa, Asia, South America, and India—rational arguments sound awfully hollow and powerless when you are confronted by a witch doctor or sorcerer possessed by supernatural power from hell!

It is becoming equally apparent to ministers in the more developed nations that mere words and arguments are often powerless in the face of devastating disease, mental problems, marital crises, and the loss of loved ones. Today as never before, the world desperately needs the bona fide ministry of the apostle with the confirmation of God's Word through miracles, signs, and wonders. Like the apostle Paul, it is time for the apostolic ministry to come forth in power as well as in word:

> *And my speech and my preaching was not with enticing words of man's wisdom, but in demonstration of the Spirit and of power: that your faith should not stand in*

the wisdom of men, but in the power of God (1 Corinthians 2:4-5).

And by the hands of the apostles were many signs and wonders wrought among the people (Acts 5:12a).

And fear came upon every soul: and many wonders and signs were done by the apostles (Acts 2:43).

By stretching forth thine hand to heal; and that signs and wonders may be done by the name of thy holy child Jesus (Acts 4:30).

What is meant by the words, *signs*, *wonders*, and *mighty deeds* in the Scriptures? A *sign* is an outward demonstration of strength, ability, or power. To give a *sign* is to signify, to indicate, and to make known the supernatural authority and power of the sovereign God.

A *wonder* can be defined by the descriptive word itself. Simply put, a *wonder* is "any thing that makes you wonder." A *wonder* is something so strange that it causes it to be watched or observed as the portent or indication of a miracle. A *wonder* attracts the attention of the saved and unsaved alike and prompts them to respond in faith.

The term, *mighty deeds*, speaks of an inherent power residing in a thing or person by virtue of its nature, and they are manifested by the power exerted or put forth. When the apostle Paul performed miracles in the course of his ministry, he earned the attention and respect of his hearers. There is a need today for the manifestation of signs and wonders on a larger scale. As God continues to establish this apostolic movement, we are going to witness more and more signs, wonders, and miracles.

Only the Real Can Counter the Counterfeit

Even him, whose coming is after the working of Satan with all power and signs and lying wonders (2 Thessalonians 2:9).

The enemy also uses all kinds of counterfeit miracles, signs, and wonders to deceive those who are perishing. In South America, Asia, and Africa, it doesn't take the gift of discernment to know this is true. The genuine evil power of Satan and his servants is openly evident in these places. It is for this reason that many times the greatest harvest comes after the chief witch doctor or occultist in the region is confronted and defeated by the Holy Spirit in a supernatural showdown of power and authority in the spirit realm. The counterfeit will be exposed and defeated more and more through the ministry of apostles and apostolic people before the Lord returns.

"Suffering"—Not the #1 Sermon Topic

Suffering for the sake of Jesus and the Church has never been a topic or activity that draws the big crowds, but it always attracts the attention of One to whom it matters very much. The early Church fathers considered life's greatest honor to die for the sake of Christ in martyrdom, but "modern Church fathers" seem to consider it life's greatest disappointment. Paul wrote:

And whether we be afflicted, it is for your consolation and salvation, which is effectual in the enduring of the same sufferings which we also suffer: or whether we be comforted, it is for your consolation and salvation. And our hope of you is stedfast, knowing, that as ye are partakers of the sufferings, so shall ye be also of the consolation (2 Corinthians 1:6-7).

God gives true apostles a certain grace to be able to suffer and experience suffering for the sake of the gospel. Just as pioneers on every continent and in every field of endeavor know that they will have to endure difficulties and challenges few others will ever know in order to achieve their goals, so apostles know that their calling will inevitably bring them into suffering for Christ's sake. The grace of God, which is His strength, enables them to endure all kinds of hardship and pain.

> *Are they Hebrews? so am I. Are they Israelites? so am I. Are they the seed of Abraham? so am I. Are they ministers of Christ? (I speak as a fool) I am more; in labours more abundant, in stripes above measure, in prisons more frequent, in deaths oft. Of the Jews five times received I forty stripes save one. Thrice was I beaten with rods, once was I stoned, thrice I suffered shipwreck, a night and a day I have been in the deep; in journeyings often, in perils of waters, in perils of robbers, in perils by mine own countrymen, in perils by the heathen, in perils in the city, in perils in the wilderness, in perils in the sea, in perils among false brethren; in weariness and painfulness, in watchings often, in hunger and thirst, in fastings often, in cold and nakedness. Beside those things that are without, that which cometh upon me daily, the care of all the churches* (2 Corinthians 11:22-28).

Personal Call, Corporate Commission

As with each of the five *doma* gifts given to the Church by Jesus, the apostle must receive a personal call into lifelong service directly from God. The apostle's call is all-encompassing and lifelong; it is a call to service, not lordship. There can be no exception to this guideline set forth by the Word of God: The true apostle has received a call directly from God.

In a measure even more extensive than with the prophet, evangelist, pastor, or teacher, the apostle's commission or sanctification (being set apart for a holy purpose) and sending is a corporate act, inspired by the Holy Spirit and confirmed through many hearts bearing witness. The apostle is called personally and set apart corporately.

> *As they ministered to the Lord, and fasted, the Holy Ghost said, Separate Me Barnabas and Saul for the work whereunto I have called them. And when they had fasted and prayed, and laid their hands on them, they sent them away. So they, being sent forth by the Holy Ghost, departed unto Seleucia; and from thence they sailed to Cyprus* (Acts 13:2-4).

The twelve apostles of the Lamb and Paul, an apostle by direct revelation, were personally called by the Lord. The Twelve were called personally by Jesus while He was on the earth. Paul was called through a vision after Jesus had already ascended to the Father. These were the apostles of the "first order," the apostles ordained and anointed to bear witness personally to the things Jesus did and said. After that there were the apostles of the Church, such as Barnabas and others. Each of them, as with today's apostles, were personally called by the Holy Spirit. Apostles must "know that they know" that they are called by God.

Jesus was *sent* by the Father according to John's Gospel, and the Twelve were sent by Jesus. Likewise, Paul and the New Testament apostles were sent by the Holy Spirit through the Church elders and the local church bodies at large.

The Apostle's Seal

*Am I not an apostle? am I not free? have I not seen
Jesus Christ our Lord? are not ye my work in the Lord?
If I be not an apostle unto others, yet doubtless I am to
you: for the seal of mine apostleship are ye in the Lord*
(1 Corinthians 9:1-2).

Paul was saying two things: "I am an apostle," and "*You
are my work* and *the seal of my apostleship*." The people
whose lives are touched by an apostle literally become the
"seal" or "proof positive" of his call and ministry effectiveness. They become the summer or fall harvest that is incon-
trovertible proof of a farmer's diligent labors earlier in the
spring.

According to *Thayer's*, one of the key definitions of "seal"
is "that by which anything is confirmed, proved, authenticat-
ed, as by a seal (a token or proof)."[1] Validity of Paul's apostleship was confirmed by the very fact that Paul had founded
the church in Corinth; he had personally won many of them
to the Lord and had grounded them in the Word of God. The
saints who came to know the Lord and the churches that were
founded through the apostle were the inscription, sign, and
seal that confirmed Paul's apostleship. The same is true today.

True Apostles Are Humble

This principle was illustrated by the High Apostle of our
faith, Jesus Christ, as Paul noted in his letter to the church at
Philippi: "And being found in fashion as a man, he humbled
himself, and became obedient unto death, even the death of the
cross" (Phil. 2:8). The Book of Proverbs tells us, "The fear of
the Lord is the instruction of wisdom; and before honour is
humility" (Prov. 15:33); "Before destruction the heart of man
is haughty, and before honour is humility" (Prov. 18:12); and

"By humility and the fear of the Lord are riches, and honour, and life" (Prov. 22:4).

The apostles of the Church today are to act no differently than the high priest of our profession, Christ Jesus (see Heb. 3:1). The only begotten Son of God, the Lord of lords and King of kings, willingly humbled Himself before God the Father and became obedient unto death, even the death of the cross (see Phil. 2:8). So why would we think that we can do anything differently? We certainly aren't holier or more deserving that the Son of God, who openly displayed humility and willingly went to the cross. Humility was a result of the obedience of Christ's action. The Scriptures are filled with this godly virtue of humility demonstrated in the life of Christ, of His apostles, and of other leaders in the Bible.

Take my yoke upon you, and learn of me; for I am meek and lowly in heart: and ye shall find rest unto your souls. For my yoke is easy, and my burden is light (Matthew 11:29-30).

Blessed are the poor in spirit: for theirs is the kingdom of heaven. Blessed are they that mourn: for they shall be comforted. Blessed are the meek: for they shall inherit the earth. Blessed are they which do hunger and thirst after righteousness: for they shall be filled (Matthew 5:3-6).

Perhaps the most graphic description of the life of an apostle in the first century was penned by the apostle Paul in his first letter to the Corinthians:

For I think that God hath set forth us the apostles last, as it were appointed to death: for we are made a spectacle unto the world, and to angels, and to men. We are fools for Christ's sake, but ye are wise in Christ; we are weak, but ye are strong; ye are honorable, but we are despised. Even unto this present hour we both hunger, and thirst, and are naked, and are buffeted, and have no certain dwellingplace; and labour, working with our own hands: being reviled, we bless; being perse-cuted, we suffer it: being defamed, we intreat: we are made as the filth of the world, and are the offscouring of all things unto this day. I write not these things to shame you, but as my beloved sons I warn you. For though ye have ten thousand instructors in Christ, yet have ye not many fathers: for in Christ Jesus I have begotten you through the gospel. Wherefore I beseech you, be ye followers of me (1 Corinthians 4:9-16).

Paul the apostle displayed the true marks of an apostle and the character of God throughout his ministry. It was this same man who stated that the apostles "were the last." Perhaps this has to do with the definition of the Greek word for humility or humble, which is *tapeinoo*. It means "to humiliate in con-dition or heart:—to abase, bring low, humble self."[2] Two other apostles had something to say about humility as well:

But he giveth more grace. Wherefore he saith, God resisteth the proud, but giveth grace unto the humble. Submit yourselves therefore to God. Resist the devil, and he will flee from you...Humble yourselves in the sight of the Lord, and he shall lift you up (James 4:6-7, 10).

Likewise, ye younger, submit yourselves unto the elder. Yea, all of you be subject one to another, and be clothed with humility: for God resisteth the proud, and giveth grace to the humble. Humble yourselves therefore under the mighty hand of God, that he may exalt you in due time (1 Peter 5:5-6).

True Apostles Have the Spirit of a Servant

Have you ever noticed that all the apostles spoke of themselves as "bond slaves" of Jesus Christ? Paul wrote, "Paul, a servant of Jesus Christ, called to be an apostle, separated unto the gospel of God" (Rom. 1:1); and, "Paul and Timotheus, the servants of Jesus Christ..." (Phil. 1:1).

The spirit of our day is, "Serve *me* and meet *my* demands. I am first; meet my needs." Paul, Peter, and John were not dictators or lords over God's heritage. They understood that the greatest among them was the one who was a servant (see Matt. 23:11).

Passing the Baton

Every church leader, and apostles in particular, should want their ministry to *outlive* their generation. With this view in mind, every spiritual father should look for one of his spiritual sons to take his vision and ministry to the next generation. No matter how anointed we may be, there will come a time when we will have to depart from the center stage of our ministry and ultimately from this earth (should the Lord tarry).

Most ministries today die out and fade away after one generation because no provision was made to extend the ministry to the next generation. When the leader departs, the ministry immediately fails for lack of a leader. In essence, everything that the minister worked for and built in his life deteriorates and is destroyed in a couple of weeks or months. This is *not* the biblical model handed down to us by Jesus, by Moses, by Abraham, Isaac, and Joseph, and by the apostles of the first century.

Looking Ahead of the Journey

Every leader should want to *reproduce himself* through other men and women given to him by the Lord. The spiritual sons and daughters whom God brings into your life and ministry are there to carry on the *ministry of the Lord*. In the final analysis, your calling, vision, and goals should come from and be empowered by God Himself. If they aren't, then don't worry about helping those things outlive you—they *need* to die. Consider the many examples before us.

Jesus and the Twelve

Jesus trained the Twelve with the view of them succeeding Him and accomplishing the fullness of that which began in the heart of the Father. Jesus planted Himself in the earth as the Eternal Seed, and He fully expected His disciples to come along after He rose from the earth to reap what He had sown. The Father's dream spanned countless generations, but it began and found its expression through His Son's perfect obedience, which in turn flowed through the Twelve, and thence to all who would believe and be joined to His Church.

Moses and Joshua

Just before his death, Moses laid his hands on Joshua and publicly ordained and commissioned him with great encouragement to take up the leadership mantle and lead the people of Israel into the Promised Land. Moses instructed him in all that he knew and encouraged Joshua to follow God's Word wholeheartedly.

And Joshua the son of Nun was full of the spirit of wisdom; for Moses had laid his hands upon him: and the children of Israel hearkened unto him, and did as the Lord commanded Moses (Deuteronomy 34:9).

Paul and Timothy

The apostle Paul did the same thing. He hoped to provide solid leadership for the churches he had founded because he knew that he was likely to lose his life in the work of the Lord:

Thou therefore, my son, be strong in the grace that is in Christ Jesus. And the things that thou hast heard of me among many witnesses, the same commit thou to faithful men, who shall be able to teach others also (2 Timothy 2:1-2).

When Paul was imprisoned in Rome (a period that would end in his death), he left behind him many fully trained, ministry-seasoned, and dedicated spiritual sons, including Timothy, John Mark, Titus, and others. These young men continued to minister in the many churches birthed through Paul's faithful apostolic ministry. When the church at Jerusalem was scattered, that left primarily the churches founded or co-founded by Paul to carry on the work of spreading the good news from bases in city-churches throughout Asia Minor.

The Spiritual Father Who Hated His Son

There is one glaring example of a God-ordained leader who openly fought against his successor, and his end will be remembered eternally as an example of a spiritual father who found himself in direct opposition to God's declared will. I'm talking, of course, about Saul, the King of Israel.

In First Samuel 18:2, the Bible says, "And Saul took him that day, and would let him go no more home to his father's house." In other words, the king adopted young David as his own son and later promoted him over the men of war. Yet when God's favor caused David to win more praise from the people than Saul did, the king became envious and jealous and sought to kill David. God Himself intervened and brought Saul to an untimely and violent death, and He promoted David to the thrones of both Judah and Israel.

David wisely prepared his son, Solomon, to take the baton next. The first and highest priority he passed along to his son was the importance of honoring God and building His house wisely. Like King David, we need to understand that the future of our ministry and of the Church is dependent on a successor.

Dear leader, does your ministry have a legacy? Does it have a future? Does it have a successor? Are you hounding your successor, or are you carefully pouring yourself into a God-chosen Joshua or Timothy in the house?[3] Wisdom calls you to prepare spiritual sons so they will skillfully and wisely take the ministry higher and will faithfully take the baton of apostolic anointing from your hand and carry it to the next generation.

Endnotes

1. Carl L.W. Grimm, *A Greek-English Lexicon of the New Testament*, trans., rev., and enl. by Joseph Henry Thayer (Grand Rapids, MI: Baker Book House, 1970, 1977).

2. James Strong, *Strong's Exhaustive Concordance of the Bible* (Peabody, MA: Hendrickson Publishers, n.d.), **humble** (#G5013).

3. The best situation of all is for you to raise up your own physical sons and daughters with such a heart for God that they are *also* spiritual sons and daughters. Thus they will be well equipped and prepared to assume more than the "legal" or outward reins of your ministry or calling. Unfortunately, many of the children of great

men of God in the past have not been spiritual off-spring and quickly destroyed or wasted everything their fathers and mothers had worked to build over a lifetime of sacrifice. As we've noted before, true fatherhood (in the natural and in the spiritual) begins at home, and it forms the foundation for every work done outside the home.

Chapter 9

Apostolic Warfare and the Laying On of Hands

What is apostolic warfare? The first thing to understand is that it is *not* natural warfare between physical entities. It is by definition a specialized form of *spiritual warfare* unique to the gifts, perceptions, and God-given grace of apostles and apostolic people. Spiritual warfare is the process of discerning, confronting, and defeating supernatural beings who control the world's systems and ideologies while strongly influencing, controlling, or oppressing the people of the earth.

I grew up in what has been called "a developing nation," and I can tell you that most converts in my homeland of South Africa come into the Church through *signs and wonders*. On the other hand, the concept of spiritual warfare has only *begun* to be considered an accepted practice in the western countries. Leaders such as Dr. C. Peter Wagner and others in the West have documented the effectiveness of such strategies as "spiritual mapping" and aggressive intercessory prayer to open the heavens over nations in South America and elsewhere, and I applaud their labors. Yet these things have been known and practiced in the "third world" for centuries.

The problem goes all the way back to the ancient Greek philosophers and their considerable influence over Roman culture and, ultimately, the Church. Although I consider logic and the ability to think analytically to be a gift from God, I do not believe that we should worship logic and reason as the sole source of knowledge and wisdom in the universe. The truth is that they are not.

While the West is more "rational" in its approach to spiritual matters;[1] people in the Far East, in Africa, and in South America see the need for warfare on *all levels*. Many of the same differences existed between the Jews and Greeks. The Greeks were philosophers who demanded arguments and proofs and valued them above all other things (although they were also very superstitious), while the Jews wanted signs of the supernatural God. The problem is that whether you were born in Jerusalem or Athens; in Kinshasa, Zaire, or the U.S.A.; God's Word is true. We must conform to God's plan, not the other way around.

The Book of Ephesians presents seven portraits of the Church, the people of God. These portraits include her function as a family, as a temple, and as the Bride of Christ. However, the final picture of the people of God in Ephesians is that of an *army*.

Before the foundation of the earth, celestial war broke out in the heavens. In the twinkling of an eye, one third of the angels in Heaven were cast down to the earth along with their fallen archangel, Lucifer:

And there was war in heaven: Michael and his angels fought against the dragon…. And the great dragon was cast out, that old serpent, called the Devil, and Satan, which deceiveth the whole world: he was cast out into the earth, and his angels were cast out with him (Revelation 12:7,9).

Satan has declared war on our Father and His children. Although he is a defeated foe, it is still our job to "clean up" his evil works and workers operating in the earth.

This war is of global proportion, and our Father is the Creator, whose power and wisdom are beyond measure or description. According to Exodus 15:3, "The Lord is a man of war: the Lord is his name." Just as our God and Father is a "man of war," so His family has been given His "DNA"— manifested supernaturally through the spirit to wage war against evil princes. This is the reason that the people of God are so often pictured as *soldiers.* (The apostle Paul takes for granted that all Christians are involved in this war.)

Thou therefore endure hardness, as a good soldier of Jesus Christ. No man that warreth entangleth himself with the affairs of this life; that he may please him who hath chosen him to be a soldier (2 Timothy 2:3-4).

Fight the good fight of faith, lay hold on eternal life, whereunto thou art also called, and hast professed a good profession before many witnesses (1 Timothy 6:12).

The True Nature of the Conflict

The apostle Paul described the scope of the conflict and its nature in his letter to the church at Ephesus:

Finally, my brethren, be strong in the Lord, and in the power of his might. Put on the whole armour of God, that ye may be able to stand against the wiles of the devil. For we wrestle not against flesh and blood, but against principalities, against powers, against the rulers of the darkness of this world, against spiritual wickedness in high places (Ephesians 6:10-12).

The Control of the World and Its Condition

In John's Gospel, we are told that the whole world is under the influence of the evil one (see John 3:19). According to Paul's detailed descriptions of the hierarchy of the enemy in Ephesians 6, the world (which is not so much the planet Earth, but the territory ruled by "the prince of the power of the air" [Eph. 2:2]) and its various components within the sciences, economics, and human political systems, are organized by high-ranking evil spirits who govern territories and jurisdictions of the earth.

Many events that shape human history have been influenced in unseen ways by powerful and evil supernatural beings in the heavenlies (not in Heaven, the abode of God, but in the lower heavens still beyond our sight). Various human cultures and peoples of the earth have given Satan powerful footholds in their governments and future through acts of corporate sin that, historically, have opened the door to satanic powers.

None of this has caught God "off guard" or by surprise. He has seen it all, and He measured its full weight in store for final judgment. Most importantly, God has had a plan of salvation and restoration for the earth even longer than the earth has existed (embodied in His Son, the Sacrificed Lamb "slain from the foundation of the world" [Rev. 13:8])!

Therefore, *it is no accident* that He is raising up apostles and apostolic people in this day to lead God's people in dethroning these ancient principalities by apostolic binding and losing in concert with the Body of Christ bonded together in true unity. Matthew's Gospel explains the nature of this warfare in graphic terms: "And from the days of John the Baptist until now the kingdom of heaven suffereth violence, and *the violent take it by force*" (Matt. 11:12).

The apostolic (or "sent") people of God are becoming the "ruling territorial spirits of the land" under God's leadership. For too long the Church has functioned out of a *passive* mindset and spirit. *We have been on the defensive for centuries, but now it is time for us to become* **confrontational** *and* **violent** *against the hordes of hell.* (Notice that I said "against the hordes of hell," not against flesh and blood or people.)

Included in our true apostolic commission is the divine authority and power to dethrone evil princes and *replace them* through the planting of new churches as the Kingdom of God advances relentlessly across national borders, spiritual boundaries, and forbidden zones formerly dominated by the enemy! The "embassy" or heavenly base from which His ambassadors attack is the apostolic commission.

The Bible contains many examples of times and situations in which our spiritual brothers and family knew what was ahead by God's grace and successfully confronted these spirits. Wisdom tells us to examine and take into account the key strategies that these pioneers of the faith used to defeat the enemy in the cities where they preached.

Daniel: His Words of Intercession Were Heard in Heaven

Daniel was a champion of God, a leader who battled for his nation *on his knees* in true spiritual warfare. One particular year, Daniel received an alarming prophetic insight from God; he knew that his people were in such danger that only God's divine intervention could save them. He fasted and prayed for 21 days until finally an angel of the Lord came to him:

Then said he unto me, Fear not, Daniel: for from the first day that thou didst set thine heart to understand,

103

and to chasten thyself before thy God, thy words were heard, and I am come for thy words. But the prince of the kingdom of Persia withstood me one and twenty days: but, lo, Michael, one of the chief princes, came to help me; and I remained there with the kings of Persia. Now I am come to make thee understand what shall befall thy people in the latter days: for yet the vision is for many days (Daniel 10:12-14).

Daniel confronted these spirits and defeated them. How? Through apostolic warfare (although Christ had not yet come, Daniel by the Spirit was able to tap into the power of God because of his intimacy with the Lord and his anointing as a prince and prophet of Israel).

Paul: Dethroned Spirits Over Cities, Confronted Territorial Spirits

The apostle Paul was the man who wrote, "For the kingdom of God is not in word, but in power" (1 Cor. 4:20). He meant what he said because he knew his Savior and dared to obey Him with apostolic authority and power.

Now while Paul waited for them at Athens, his spirit was stirred in him, when he saw the city wholly given to idolatry. Therefore disputed he in the synagogue with the Jews, and with the devout persons, and in the market daily with them that met with him. Then certain philosophers of the Epicureans, and of the Stoicks, encountered him... (Acts 17:16-18).

The city of Athens was given over to the spirits of numerous idols—yes, even though Athens was supposedly renowned as the center of logic and was the point of origin for Platonism, Epicurianism, Stoicism, and many more Greek philosophies, as well as the myriad of modern philosophies that have borrowed their basic ideas. (Very little is really "new.")

Paul the apostle was anointed to pioneer the work of God right in the middle of the city that ultimately provided the philosophical grounds for many modern atheists and agnostics. He was fearless in the cause of Christ, though it made him many enemies.

*For a certain man named Demetrius, a silversmith which made silver shrines for Diana, brought no small gain unto the craftsmen; whom he called together with the workmen of like occupation, and said, Sirs, ye know that by this craft we have our wealth. Moreover ye see and hear, that not alone at Ephesus, but almost throughout all Asia, this **Paul hath persuaded and turned away much people**, saying that they be no gods, which are made with hands: so that not only this our craft is in danger to be set at nought; but also that the temple of the great goddess Diana should be despised, and her magnificence should be destroyed, whom all Asia and the world worshippeth* (Acts 19:24-27).

Apostles are called and anointed to be the forerunners, the pioneers who venture into the enemy's own territory and demand God's goods—the souls of the lost and searching:

And when they had gone through the isle unto Paphos, they found a certain sorcerer, a false prophet, a Jew, whose name was Barjesus: which was with the deputy of the country, Sergius Paulus, a prudent man; who called for Barnabas and Saul, and desired to hear the word of God. But Elymas the sorcerer (for so is his name by interpretation) withstood them, seeking to turn away the deputy from the faith. Then Saul, (who also is called Paul,) filled with the Holy Ghost, set his eyes on him, and said, O full of all subtlety and all mis-chief, thou child of the devil, thou enemy of all righ-teousness, wilt thou not cease to pervert the right ways of the Lord? And now, behold, the hand of the Lord is upon thee, and thou shalt be blind, not seeing the sun for a season. And immediately there fell on him a mist and a darkness; and he went about seeking some to lead him by the hand. Then the deputy, when he saw what was done, believed, being astonished at the doc-trine of the Lord (Acts 13:6-12).

When Bar-Jesus dared to interfere with the work of the Holy Spirit in the procounsul's heart, Paul rose up in apostolic authority and boldly confronted the evil spirit who was really behind the act of interference. There was no refuting or escaping the authority Paul wielded as God's anointed apostle. In effect, Paul's apostolic anointing totally defeated and bullied the territorial spirit that had tried to rise up against the Spirit of Jesus at work in Paul. The Holy Spirit literally made the blinding of Bar-Jesus a *sign and wonder*, and it confiscated the territory that was once Satan's and made it the Lord's!

Divine Strategies, Supernatural Battle Plans

The first order of military intelligence is this: Know who your enemy is. Determine his strengths and weaknesses and understand his motives and strategies. Then you can make plans based on facts instead of guesses.

For Christians, and especially for apostles and apostolic people, our first rule is this: *The real battle is spiritual*, not physical. Therefore, the real battle takes place in the heaven-lies against spiritual forces, not on earth among mere men. The apostle Paul wrote, "For we wrestle not against flesh and blood, but against principalities, against powers, against the rulers of the darkness of this world, against spiritual wickedness in high places" (Eph. 6:12).

The source of our problem is not flesh and blood. We need to remember that the enemy of our souls expresses himself through human ideologies, philosophy, religion, sin, the occult, and other means—means through which he can express and live out his evil desires.

Seek God Afresh for His Strategy

We have already examined the battle strategy that God gave King Jehoshaphat of Judah, who called a fast and prayed when three powerful enemies came to destroy his nation. In his case, the Lord told him to have the people of God begin to sing praises to God, and the Lord laid an ambush for the enemy. Every battle may not require the same strategy. The answer is simple: *First seek the Lord* for His battle plan, "for the battle is the Lord's" (1 Sam. 17:47).

The Ministry of Angels

Throughout the New Testament record, the assignment and movement of angels accompanied the warfare prayers of the apostles. The Bible clearly teaches that angels are often sent to intervene in the affairs of nations in response to the prayers of the saints and the ministry of the apostles.

Chapter 10 of the Book of Acts tells us the miraculous story of the almost simultaneous *angelic visitations* to the apostle Peter in Joppa and to Cornelius, the Roman centurion from Italy, and how the two were brought together by divine appointment. It was with Cornelius' household that God chose to fully reveal to the Jewish church at Jerusalem just how complete Jesus' work on the cross really was—His shed blood and broken body had purchased forgiveness and eternal life *for all men* regardless of race, color, nationality, or social status!

The twelfth chapter of the Book of Acts records the miraculous intervention of *angels* to free Peter from Herod's prison in response to the apostolic congregation in the church at Jerusalem. They sought the Lord fervently and *continuously* in one heart and mind for the release of Peter, and God immediately dispatched an angelic messenger to bring their request to pass. The result was that even greater glory was given to God and His Son, Jesus Christ.

(Shortly after that, God once again dispatched an angel to invade Herod's "territory." Only this time, it was to strike Herod dead for daring to blaspheme by demanding that the Jews of Tyre and Sidon worship him as a god. It doesn't pay to interfere with the work of the apostles of the Lord, or to presume to accept or demand the worship of men....)

This is not a book on angels; however, we need to understand their role in helping the Church in the battle for souls in our fallen world. Angels are created spirit beings who are able to change their appearance. We also know that they can speak and can become visible if God allows them to. At times their appearance, demeanor, and actions will be so "normal" that we will not even realize their true nature or identity unless God reveals it to us (see Heb. 13:2).

The primary purposes or functions of angels include (but are not limited to) providing continual ministry to God the Father in round-the-clock praise, worship, and adoration in His presence and serving as messengers from His throne to people on earth. (The word *angel* is derived from the Greek word *angelos*, which means "messenger.")

The Book of Hebrews says of them, "Are they not all ministering spirits, sent forth to minister for them who shall be heirs of salvation?" (Heb. 1:14) It is interesting to note that

Christ received angelic ministry on several occasions (see Mark 1:13; Luke 22:43), and that what may be called "guardian angels" rejoice every time a sinner repents (see Luke 15:10). (In other words, angels *are watching over you and I* at all times—even before we are saved.)

According to the Bible record, it is right to conclude that angels war on behalf of the saints and that they serve as God's messengers and guardians over His people. Because angels figure so prominently in the supernatural ministry of apostles and apostolic teams of fivefold ministers, I feel that I need to briefly cover the chief ways angels may work in our lives as we pioneer new works for our King and Lord, Jesus Christ:

1. Angels protect from danger.

> *Then the high priest rose up, and all they that were with him, (which is the sect of the Sadducees,) and were filled with indignation, and laid their hands on the apostles, and put them in the common prison. **But the angel of the Lord by night opened the prison doors, and brought them forth**, and said, Go, stand and speak in the temple to the people all the words of this life* (Acts 5:17-20).

> *And when the servant of the man of God was risen early, and gone forth, behold, an host compassed the city both with horses and chariots. And his servant said unto him, Alas, my master! how shall we do? And he answered, Fear not: for **they that be with us are more than they that be with them**. And Elisha prayed, and said, Lord, I pray thee, open his eyes, that he may see. And the Lord opened the eyes of the young man; and he saw: and, behold, the mountain was full of horses and chariots of fire round about Elisha* (2 Kings 6:15-17).

2. Angels deliver God's people.

    And when Herod would have brought him forth, the same night Peter was sleeping between two soldiers, bound with two chains: and the keepers before the door kept the prison. And, behold, the angel of the Lord came upon him, and a light shined in the prison: and he smote Peter on the side, and raised him up, saying, Arise up quickly. And his chains fell off from his hands (Acts 12:6-7).

3. Angels bring messages from God to His people.

    And, lo, the angel of the Lord came upon them, and the glory of the Lord shone round about them: and they were sore afraid. And the angel said unto them, Fear not: for, behold, I bring you good tidings of great joy, which shall be to all people. For unto you is born this day in the city of David a Saviour, which is Christ the Lord. And this shall be a sign unto you; Ye shall find the babe wrapped in swaddling clothes, lying in a manger. And suddenly there was with the angel a multitude of the heavenly host praising God... (Luke 2:9-13).

4. Angels renew our strength.

    Saying, Father, if thou be willing, remove this cup from me: nevertheless not my will, but thine, be done. And there appeared an angel unto him from heaven, strengthening him. And being in an agony he prayed more earnestly: and His sweat was as it were great drops of blood falling down to the ground (Luke 22:42-44).

5. Angels fight on our behalf in the heavenlies.

    And he said unto me, O Daniel, a man greatly beloved, understand the words that I speak unto thee, and stand *upright: for unto thee am I now sent. And when he had spoken this word unto me, I stood trembling. Then said he unto me, Fear not, Daniel: for from the first day that thou didst set thine heart to understand, and to chasten thyself before thy God, thy words were heard, and **I am come for thy words**. But **the prince of the kingdom of Persia withstood me** one and twenty days: but, lo, **Michael, one of the chief princes, came to help me**; and I remained there with the kings of Persia* (Daniel 10:11-13).

6. Angels minister to us (just as they ministered to Jesus and Elijah).

   Are they not all ministering spirits, sent forth to minister for them who shall be heirs of salvation? (Hebrews 1:14)

Many times God's people don't even realize or know that they have been supernaturally protected, delivered, guided, strengthened, fought for, or ministered to by angels. It is important for us to remember that God has given angels to us (as His saints) to assist us in our warfare against the evil powers and to thank Him for them.

The Key to Apostolic Warfare

The most important thing for us to remember in the apostolic ministry is that the battle isn't ours to win or lose—Christ Jesus has already *defeated* the enemy: "And having spoiled principalities and powers, he made a show of them openly, triumphing over them in it" (Col. 2:15).

Satan and his hordes of fallen angels have *already* been disarmed and rendered powerless through the voluntary death of Jesus Christ on the cross and His resurrection from the dead. Let us continue to enforce the victory gained for us by our Lord, Jesus Christ.

The Apostle and the Laying On of Hands

The New Testament apostles believed that when they laid their hands on the saints and other workers, an actual *impartation* took place in their lives. They clearly imparted healing, activated gifts and callings, and ordained and sanctioned the call of the believers with apostolic authority.

The views of the early apostles were clearly influenced by the importance attached to the laying on of hands in the Old Testament. Joseph even differentiated between the right and the left hand in the level of impartation each carried when he brought his two sons to Jacob for a "father's blessing" (see Gen. 48:13-14). The right hand in that culture was considered to be the hand of power in blessing as well as in warfare (when wielding a sword or spear). The New Testament reveals several key purposes or benefits that were imparted through the laying on of hands.

The Laying On of Hands Was Done:

1. To impart blessings.

   For I [Paul] *long to see you, that I may impart unto you some spiritual gift, to the end ye may be established* (Romans 1:11).

2. To minister signs and wonders.

   And by the hands of the apostles were many signs and wonders wrought among the people; (and they were all with one accord in Solomon's porch (Acts 5:12).

3. To minister the baptism of the Holy Spirit.

   Now when the apostles which were at Jerusalem heard that Samaria had received the word of God, they sent unto them Peter and John: who, when they were come down, prayed for them, that they might receive the Holy Ghost: (for as yet he was fallen upon none of them: only they were baptized in the name of the Lord Jesus.) Then laid they their hands on them, and they received the Holy Ghost (Acts 8:14-17).

4. To impart spiritual gifts (as listed in First Corinthians 12).

Wherefore I put thee in remembrance that thou stir up the gift of God, which is in thee by the putting on of my hands (2 Timothy 1:6).

5. To ordain ministers of the gospel.

Whom they set before the apostles: and when they had prayed, they laid their hands on them (Acts 6:6).

And Joshua the son of Nun was full of the spirit of wisdom; for Moses had laid his hands upon him: and the children of Israel hearkened unto him, and did as the Lord commanded Moses (Deuteronomy 34:9).

Neglect not the gift that is in thee, which was given thee by prophecy, with the laying on of the hands of the presbytery (1 Timothy 4:14).

6. To commission and send forth.

And when they had fasted and prayed, and laid their hands on them, they sent them away. So they, being sent forth by the Holy Ghost, departed unto Seleucia... (Acts 13:3-4).

And the Lord said unto Moses, Take thee Joshua the son of Nun, a man in whom is the spirit, and lay thine hand upon him; and set him before Eleazar the priest, and before all the congregation; and give him a charge in their sight. And thou shalt put some of thine honor upon him, that all the congregation of the children of Israel may be obedient (Numbers 27:18-20).

For obvious reasons, the laying on of hands was an integral part of the early Church as well as part of the ancient practices of Israel. According to chapter 6 of the Book of Hebrews, the laying on of hands was one of the elementary and therefore foundational doctrines and practices of the apostles in the first century. In summary, the apostles laid hands on people to impart blessings, minister signs and wonders, baptize in the Holy Spirit, impart spiritual gifts, and to ordain and commission the saints for separated service unto God and His people.

The Apostles' Doctrine

Although it may not appear to be as "exciting" as casting out devils or healing the sick of fatal diseases, the apostles also conducted warfare with *the truth* in the form of "the apostles' doctrine."

*Then Peter said unto them, Repent, and be baptized every one of you in the name of Jesus Christ for the remission of sins, and ye shall receive the gift of the Holy Ghost. For the promise is unto you, and to your children, and to all that are afar off, even as many as the Lord our God shall call. And with many other words did he testify and exhort, saying, Save yourselves from this untoward generation. Then they that gladly received his word were baptized: and the same day there were added unto them about three thousand souls. **And they continued stedfastly in the apostles' doctrine** and fellowship, and in breaking of bread, and in prayers. And fear came upon every soul: and many wonders and signs were done by the apostles* (Acts 2:38-43).

114

The Greek word translated as "doctrine" is *didache*, and it means "teaching or that which is taught."[2] In an age filled with dangerous heresies and half-truths about Christ and God's Kingdom, the apostles' doctrine became the backbone of the rapidly growing Church. In Hebrews chapter 6, the apostles' doctrine is revealed as the foundational doctrines of Christ, the Chief Cornerstone.

These fundamental teachings became a firm anchor of orthodoxy in a storm-tossed sea of anti-Christ movements, Gnostic heresy that denied the physical death and resurrection of Christ, Greek philosophies that almost totally denied the existence of the spirit realm, and pagan religions that appealed to the fleshly appetites without fear of punishment for sin. The key teachings of the apostles covered five key subjects.

1. The deity of Jesus Christ.

    This doctrine was and is perhaps the most important of all the doctrines in the Christian faith.

    [God] *hath in these last days spoken unto us by his Son, whom he hath appointed heir of all things, by whom also he made the worlds; who being the brightness of his glory, and the express image of his person, and upholding all things by the word of his power, when he had by himself purged our sins, sat down on the right hand of the Majesty on high* (Hebrews 1:2-3).

    In the beginning was the Word, and the Word was with God, and the Word was God. The same was in the beginning with God. All things were made by him; and without him was not any thing made that was made (John 1:1-3).

    And without controversy great is the mystery of godliness: God was manifest in the flesh, justified in the

Spirit, seen of angels, preached unto the Gentiles, believed on in the world, received up into glory (1 Timothy 3:16).

The apostles preached the centrality of Christ in all things. They instructed the Church concerning His virgin birth, sinless life, miracles, teachings, death, burial, resurrection, and ascension to the Father. Jesus Christ was boldly declared to be the express image of the invisible God, God incarnate, and the only begotten Son of God come in the flesh.

2. The preaching of the cross.

For Christ sent me not to baptize, but to preach the gospel: not with wisdom of words, lest the cross of Christ should be made of none effect. For the preaching of the cross is to them that perish foolishness; but unto us which are saved it is the power of God. For it is written, I will destroy the wisdom of the wise, and will bring to nothing the understanding of the prudent. Where is the wise? where is the scribe? where is the disputer of this world? hath not God made foolish the wisdom of this world? For after that in the wisdom of God the world by wisdom knew not God, it pleased God by the foolishness of preaching to save them that believe. For the Jews require a sign, and the Greeks seek after wisdom: but we preach Christ crucified, unto the Jews a stumblingblock, and unto the Greeks foolishness; but unto them which are called, both Jews and Greeks, Christ the power of God, and the wisdom of God (1 Corinthians 1:17-24).

The preaching of the cross was the central focus of the early Church, and the gospel of Jesus Christ was preached as the power of God unto salvation. Paul did not add to the gospel, for Jesus was the source of his message. Although the preaching of the cross was seen as "foolishness" to the world, it was the wisdom of God to those who believed and were saved.

3. The resurrection of Jesus.

For I delivered unto you first of all that which I also received, how that Christ died for our sins according to the scriptures; and that he was buried, and that he rose again the third day according to the scriptures (1 Corinthians 15:3-4).

The resurrection of Jesus Christ differentiated Jesus from every other person in human history; it placed our Lord Jesus in a "class" of His own. The New Testament writers say that on the third day, Jesus—the person they personally knew and had contact with—came back from the dead. They saw Him, spoke to Him, and touched Him. They recognized His face and form, and they concluded that He was the same Jesus they had touched and known. In the end, all but one of the Twelve laid down their lives because of their belief in this risen Christ. (People don't willingly die for a lie.)

Now if Christ be preached that he rose from the dead, how say some among you that there is no resurrection of the dead? But if there be no resurrection of the dead, then is Christ not risen: and if Christ be not risen, then is our preaching vain, and your faith is also vain. Yea, and we are found false witnesses of God; because we have testified of God that he raised up Christ: whom he raised not up, if so be that the dead rise not. For if the dead rise not, then is not Christ raised: and if Christ be not raised, your faith is vain; ye are yet in your sins (1 Corinthians 15:12-17).

4. The veracity of the Scriptures.

*We have also a **more sure word of prophecy**; where-unto ye do well that ye take heed, as unto a light that shineth in a dark place, until the day dawn, and the day star arise in your hearts: knowing this first, that no prophecy of the scripture is of any private interpreta-tion. For the prophecy came not in old time by the will of man: but **holy men of God spake as they were moved by the Holy Ghost*** (2 Peter 1:19-21).

But though we, or an angel from heaven, preach any other gospel unto you than that which we have preached unto you, let him be accursed. As we said before, so say I now again, If any man preach any other gospel unto you than that ye have received, let him be accursed. For do I now persuade men, or God? or do I seek to please men? for if I yet pleased men, I should not be the servant of Christ (Galatians 1:8-10).

The apostles believed that the Scriptures (the Old Testament, or Torah, containing the Books of Moses, the Law, and the Prophets at that time) were given by inspiration of the Holy Spirit, were infallible, and were God's revealed Word to man.

5. The breaking of bread.

*And they continued stedfastly in the apostles' doctrine and fellowship, and in **breaking of bread**, and in prayers* (Acts 2:42).

The sharing of communion was something that the apostles taught and practiced, evidently every time they met. The breaking of bread reminded them of the

118

they met. The breaking of bread reminded them of the shed blood and broken body of Jesus Christ sacrificed for them according to the ordinance received from the Lord.

For I have received of the Lord that which also I delivered unto you, That the Lord Jesus the same night in which he was betrayed took bread: and when he had given thanks, he brake it, and said, Take, eat: this is my body, which is broken for you: this do in remembrance of me. After the same manner also he took the cup, when he had supped, saying, This cup is the new testament in my blood: this do ye, as oft as ye drink it, in remembrance of me. For as often as ye eat this bread, and drink this cup, ye do show the Lord's death till he come (1 Corinthians 11:23-26)

Six Attributes of God's War on Satanic Powers

Spiritual warfare is very different from natural warfare in many respects. However, there are six things God provides when He sends us into war:

1. a Divine Declaration
2. a Divine Solution
3. Divine Aid
4. Divine Direction
5. Divine Devotion
6. Divine Deposit

Endnotes

1. This *should* sound as odd to your ears as if I said, "The West is more spiritual in its approach to rational matters." The things of the Spirit can only be perceived by the Spirit. God often does speak to our minds and intellect, and we are to worship with our intellect as well.

However, the "salvation connection" can only be made "spirit to spirit"; it cannot be perceived or accomplished solely through the mind. For an excellent examination of this area, I recommend the book, *Mere Christianity* by the late C.S. Lewis (MacMillan Publishing Co., 1952).

2. James Strong, *Strong's Exhaustive Concordance of the Bible* (Peabody, MA: Hendrickson Publishers, n.d.), **doctrine** (#G1322).

Chapter 10

The Apostle and Team Ministry

The culture and philosophy of ministry in the local church in which I grew up was an imbalanced model, but it remains the model of choice for most Christian churches today. It was imbalanced because it was based on the mentality that one local church needs only one pastor.

An important consequence of this mentality and system of government is that the sole pastor of a local church is controlled by a deacon board that has the power to out-vote the pastor on almost all issues of vision and administration in the church. Many people who live under some form of democratic government often say, "Well, that doesn't sound so bad. Everybody has a vote, so what's wrong with that?"

The problem is that pastors serving under this system do not have the freedom to express their *divine* call or to implement *spiritual* guidance because deacon boards—rarely recognized

for lofty spiritual vision or insight—tend to position themselves as self-appointed "watch dogs" in opposition to the
pastor in the local church. Deacons in this setting often perceive themselves to be "employers," which effectively
reduces the pastor to a role that is abhorred throughout the
Scriptures: He was thus nothing more or less than an employ-
ee or *hireling*.

Even worse, many deacon boards consider themselves to
be "protectors" who place themselves strategically between
the pastor and the sheep to make sure their hired hand doesn't
get too heavy-handed in his ministry and leadership. This is
adversarial relationship at its very worst.

The isolated pastor must serve his local church body while
being subjected to feelings of enforced loneliness, misunder-
standing, and, worst of all, a loss of human dignity. (How
would you like to be given responsibility for some people and
then be "watched" the whole time by a committee of watch
dogs charged with protecting those people from your poten-
tially abusive ways?)

Insecurity Leads to the "Lone Ranger" Syndrome

While growing up in the church I mentioned, I noticed that
our intimidated pastor often seemed to feel insecure. As a
result, he began to live out the ministerial equivalent of the
"Lone Ranger." By that I mean he tried to be everything and
do everything for everyone. He took on the total responsibility of shepherding the flock, of counseling the hurting, of
transporting the sick to the hospital and visiting them regularly, and even driving people around and serving as the
church social worker. No one said anything because the
unspoken consensus was that "this is the job description of
the pastor."

When I accepted the call to the ministry, I naturally began to serve as a local church pastor within the framework of this same ministry model. It wasn't long before I put on my own "Lone Ranger suit" and became deeply frustrated and nearly burned out from the crushing burden of the work.

Finally I turned to the Lord and His Word for answers. The first thing I noticed is that Jesus clearly and emphatically stated that His yoke is easy and His burden is light (see Matt. 11:28-30). In Hebrews 4:9, my weariness began to lift as I was reminded that "there remaineth therefore a rest to the people of God." If I could somehow learn how to enter His rest, then I could also "cease from my labors" as Christ had from His (see Heb. 4:10).

The Scriptures pertaining to the nature of God's work and His workmen came alive with meaning. I began to understand that the pressure to lead, administer, and pastor the church *alone* was an *unbiblical model of government.* I began to understand the need for team ministry and the need for other gifted saints who were graced by the Lord to be involved with the work of the local church.

I joyfully communicated my discoveries and desires with other friends, thinking that they would all respond with affirmation. To my surprise, I was informed that this new model of team ministry would not work! My fellow pastors were startled and perplexed, primarily because team ministry was a relatively new concept and they did not see such models in their sphere of influence.

Other leaders warned me that my concept of team ministry was dangerous, because they knew of other churches that had experimented with this new model, only to experience betrayal and disorder. Overall, most of the people I talked with about team ministry had a very negative bias against it.

Reject the *Status Quo*; Embrace the *Status Dei*

I had already seen and personally experienced the unpleasant fruit of the status quo, however. I had determined that Scripture had the final say in all matters concerning the ministry and the Church. My personal study of the Scriptures had produced a final conclusion that there was sufficient evidence of team ministry in the New Testament Church. I wanted to try God's way, the "status Dei."

I was convinced that I had an obligation to teach my deacon board and congregation about the strengths of and the need for team ministry. Over a period of several months, I patiently communicated and modeled new roles and clear patterns of leadership for my leaders.

The transition to team leadership was a gradual process spread out over two years. After two years had passed, some of the leaders and members of the congregation had made the transition. Others flatly rejected this "new" philosophy of ministry (although it was the unbiblical "deacon board/ hireling pastor" system that was the new man-made system— the team leadership model was pioneered by the apostles 2,000 years ago). I then decided to leave my existing church and pioneer this concept by starting a local church.[1]

What Is Team Ministry?

You have "team ministry" whenever two or more Christians *work together* to accomplish a common God-given vision or task. A "team" in this context is a plurality of gifted people who have been identified, trained, equipped, activated, and placed or set into the local church to accomplish the God-given vision.

There is something else about team ministry that is critical to its success. Teams, as working or functional extensions or subgroupings of the Body of Christ, are more like a family or living organism than some machine or interchangeable device. I learned this the hard way when, in my zeal to see team ministry in operation, I bypassed the people with whom I had proven relationships and acquired the ministry services of two men from outside the local church.

I discovered through the hard and trying times that followed that these Christian brothers were not committed to the larger purpose of the local church. With much sorrow we had to part company. Yes, these were wonderful brothers in the Lord. But they had not been sovereignly "set" in that local body by God. They were artificially placed into leadership, and I was the culprit. They were not *called* by God to share in the responsibility of the local church.

How Do We Acquire Team Members?

After many hard lessons learned, I am convinced that team members should be raised up from the local church. I only look for those who have shown themselves to be faithful, responsible, and committed to the vision of the local church. Abram followed the same principle when he would only go out to war in the company of those born in his own household (see Gen. 14:14).

The Benefits of Team Ministry

There are five key benefits to the team ministry concept revealed in the Scriptures:

1. *Two are better than one.* "Two are better than one; because they have a good reward for their labour" (Eccles. 4:9; see also verses 10-12).

   - They have good reward for their labors.
   - There is greater safety—when one falls; the other lifts him up.

- Someone may prevail against one, but two will withstand their adversary.
- A threefold cord is not easily broken.

2. *"And five of you shall chase an hundred, and an hundred of you shall put ten thousand to flight"* (Lev. 26:8a). This speaks of corporate or team strength in times of conflict or spiritual warfare.

3. *It is God's provision for reaching the goal of Ephesians 4:12,* which is to equip the saints "...for the work of the ministry, for the edifying of the body of Christ."

4. *The Body grows and builds itself up in love.* When the saints are identified, trained, equipped, and activated to begin working in their place, the entire Body grows and is nourished in love.

> *But speaking the truth in love, may grow up into him in all things, which is the head, even Christ: from whom the whole body fitly joined together and compacted by that which every joint supplieth, according to the effectual working in the measure of every part, maketh increase of the body unto the edifying of itself in love* (Ephesians 4:15-16).

5. *The Body is stabilized and strengthened to resist every attack and deception.*

> *That we henceforth be no more children, tossed to and fro, and carried about with every wind of doctrine, by the sleight of men, and cunning craftiness, whereby they lie in wait to deceive* (Ephesians 4:14).

It is clear that both the Old and New Testaments teach and model team ministry. The growth, expansion, and strength of our vision as leaders is determined by the diversities of gifts God places under our leadership as resource material.

When people placed in the local body by God are identified and placed in their place of function, they add strength to the vision of accomplishing our God-given dreams. Through team ministry we are able to produce far greater results and productivity. Remember, every vision needs resources. The people God sends to us are His personal gifts and resources joined to us to help accomplish His vision for the body.

Fifteen Principles for Effective Team Ministry

1. *Vision.* A vision is God's revealed desire for the local church and individuals. Every individual, team, and local body has objectives that God wants us to accomplish. Proverbs 29:18 says, "Where there is no vision, the people perish: but he that keepeth the law, happy is he."

   A vision is a dream imparted by God. It gives you the conviction that there are things that must be accomplished during your lifetime. It is a divinely communicated purpose from God implanted deeply into your spirit and conscience. Your life must be dedicated to fulfill your purpose.

   Julius Caesar was an epileptic. Napoleon came from humble beginnings and was not thought to be very intelligent. Beethoven and Thomas Edison were born deaf, and Charles Dickens and Handel were handicapped. Homer was blind and Plato was a hunchback, while Sir Walter Scott was paralyzed. What gave these great individuals the stamina to overcome severe setbacks and become successful? They had an inner dream that lit a fire that could not be extinguished.

   Napoleon Hill said, "Cherish your visions and your dreams as they are the children of your soul; the blueprints of your ultimate achievements." Without vision, there can be no purpose or achievement.

2. *Faithfulness.* Team members must be faithful.

> *His lord said unto him, Well done, thou good and faithful servant: thou hast been faithful over a few things, I will make thee ruler over many things: enter thou into the joy of thy lord. He also that had received two talents came and said, Lord, thou deliveredst unto me two talents: behold, I have gained two other talents beside them. His lord said unto him, Well done, good and faithful servant; thou hast been faithful over a few things, I will make thee ruler over many things: enter thou into the joy of thy lord* (Matthew 25:21-23).

Paul wrote to the churches: "Moreover it is required in stewards, that a man be found faithful" (1 Cor. 4:2); and, "And the things that thou hast heard of me among many witnesses, the same commit thou to faithful men, who shall be able to teach others also" (2 Tim. 2:2).

We have the tendency to promote only those with personality and talents. The key to promotion is to find and promote those who have character, those who are gifted and faithful over little things. Those who have been faithful over a few things should be made ruler over much.

3. *Responsibility.* Team members must be responsible.

> *My servant Moses is not so, who is faithful in all mine house. With him will I speak mouth to mouth, even apparently, and not in dark speeches* (Numbers 12:7-8a).

Find men who are responsible and who fear God, then you can entrust to them major areas of responsibility. Teach them the ordinances and laws of God and *show* them how to walk and work responsibly. Look for these traits:

- People who have the ability.
- People who fear God.
- People who are truthful.
- People who hate covetousness.

Let them be rulers according to the ability God has given to each one. We are all responsible for the fulfilling of the vision.

4. *Accountability.* Team members must be accountable to others. "Also let the priests who came near the Lord consecrate themselves, lest the Lord break out against them" (Ex. 19:22 NKJV).

Let the people who qualify according to ability and spiritual ability be accountable to the leader concerning the matter entrusted to them. A lack of accountability allows room for independent personalities to raise up their will and sow bad seeds into the team. Such members don't really want to *serve* the leadership; rather, they seek recognition for themselves. Every team member must be accountable to the leadership for the work delegated to him or her.

5. *Loyalty.* Team members must be loyal and faithful followers of a cause.

> *And David went out to meet them, and answered and said unto them, If ye be come peaceably unto me to help me, mine heart shall be knit unto you: but if ye be come to betray me to mine enemies, seeing*

129

there is no wrong in mine hands, the God of our fathers look thereon, and rebuke it. Then the spirit came upon Amasai, who was chief of the captains, and he said, Thine are we, David, and on thy side, thou son of Jesse: peace, peace be unto thee, and peace be to thine helpers; for thy God helpeth thee. Then David received them, and made them captains of the band (1 Chronicles 12:17-18).

Yet I supposed it necessary to send to you Epaphroditus, my brother, and companion in labour, and fellowsoldier... (Philippians 2:25).

But I trust in the Lord Jesus to send Timotheus shortly unto you, that I also may be of good comfort, when I know your state. For I have no man likeminded, who will naturally care for your state. For all seek their own, not the things which are Jesus Christ's. But ye know the proof of him, that, as a son with the father, he hath served with me in the gospel (Philippians 2:19-22).

If you come to our local body with peace and loyalty to help build the corporate vision, then you will be received onto the ministry team in peace.

In team ministry, you will inevitably run into individuals who have an independent spirit. These members bring disloyalty into the open. Aaron and Miriam openly challenged the legitimate authority of Moses and proclaimed that they were equal. God established the concept of a *first* among equals. Even a team needs a leader. As Abaslom the son of David proved when he tried to steal his own father's throne, *disloyalty* is a virus that hurts the people of God, the Body of Jesus (see 2 Sam. 15).

6. *Transparency*. Team members must be transparent and open.

> *...If ye be come peaceably unto me to help me, mine heart shall be knit unto you: but if ye be come to betray me to mine enemies, seeing there is no wrong in mine hands, the God of our fathers look thereon, and rebuke it* (1 Chronicles 12:17).

David was open with the men who came to join the team. He wanted to know the motives of their hearts. (How different from the way we do things today.) Jesus warned that when sowing seed, "And some [seed] fell among thorns, and the thorns grew up and choked it, and it yielded no fruit" (Mark 4:7).

Some people are easily offended because of spiritual pride. If their ideas and gifts are not promoted by the leadership, they become offended. They will actively seek others to agree with their offense and form a rebellious group that will kill team spirit and dethrone the leaders.

7. *Submission*. A team member must be submitted to proper order and leadership. "Submitting yourselves one to another in the fear of God" (Eph. 5:21).

Our submission is threefold: to the God-ordained leaders of the team and local body, to the vision God has given, and to one another. Every member must realize that Jesus is the head of the team, and they should also submit to His delegated leadership. Submission is an attitude of the heart marked by a person's willingness to place himself under the care, protection, and guidance of those God puts over him.

Individuals who are offended give in to an artificial spirit toward the leadership. They feel offended, questioned, and undermined by almost every decision of the leaders. These individuals can no longer receive spiritual feeding and direction from the leadership. Members who do not submit to the team leadership end up in a competition with everyone on the team. Korah and his princes are the epitome of this pattern.

> *And they rose up before Moses, with certain of the children of Israel, two hundred and fifty princes of the assembly, famous in the congregation, men of renown: and they gathered themselves together against Moses and against Aaron, and said unto them, Ye take too much upon you, seeing all the congregation are holy, every one of them, and the Lord is among them: wherefore then lift ye up yourselves above the congregation of the Lord?* (Numbers 16:2-3)[2]

> *Obey them that have the rule over you, and submit yourselves: for they watch for your souls, as they that must give account, that they may do it with joy, and not with grief: for that is unprofitable for you* (Hebrews 13:17).

> *And to esteem them very highly in love for their work's sake. And be at peace among yourselves* (1 Thessalonians 5:13).

8. *Relationship and Fellowship.* Team members must be in relationship and fellowship with other believers.

> *And they continued steadfastly in the apostles' doctrine and fellowship, and in breaking of bread, and in prayers* (Acts 2:42).

> *Then Jonathan and David made a covenant, because he loved him as his own soul* (1 Samuel 18:3).

Chapter 15 of John's Gospel reveals that Jesus enjoyed three levels of friendship in His ministry: acquaintances, socialites, and covenant friends. Jesus built quality relationships with His disciples; that was how He chose to function and relate to the men He chose as ministry team members. Jesus was relational, and at one point He called His disciples "friends" and not servants (see John 15:15).

After working with several organizations and groups over the past few years, I have concluded that a team or movement cannot be built on legislation. It must be built on relationships. One of the characteristics of the first century apostles was that they were relational, and it was out of their relationships that intimacy naturally flowed. Their intimate relationships enabled and motivated them to work out their differences instead of splitting apart.

Friendships are developed through intimacy, and it helps us learn to respect other people as people and as individuals with different personalities. Relationships produce friendships marked by mutual affection and loyalty. We can rely on a friend because we know he or she will remain a friend even in disaster or in guilt.

When teams are built on intimacy and relationships, the determining factor is not ideally a purpose or a goal; it is based on unspoken but nevertheless "promised" loyalty to one another and refreshing openness. We automatically help our friends without any reward, recognition, or return favor, and we do it simply for the relationship's sake.

We must learn strategies that build our relationships and guard against individuals who would like to destroy them. Intimate relationships unite our affection and respect, and they form a firm foundation upon which we can build healthy and strong team ministries.

9. *Corporate Prayer.* There must be specified times of corporate prayer for the vision and needs of the team and the ministry.

10. *Unity.* The team member must treasure and guard unity.

> *Behold, how good and how pleasant it is for brethren to dwell together in unity!* (Psalm 133:1)

> *A perverse man sows strife, and a whisperer separates the best of friends* (Proverbs 16:28 NKJV).

> *Cast out the scoffer, and contention will leave; yes, strife and reproach will cease* (Proverbs 22:10 NKJV).

> *Now may the God of patience and comfort grant you to be like-minded toward one another, according to Christ Jesus, that you may with one mind and one mouth glorify the God and Father of our Lord Jesus Christ* (Romans 15:5-6 NKJV).

- The anointing and power of God is present when there is unity. Every ministry team must stay on their guard against things that would destroy their unity.
- Slander, competition, envy, and jealousy must always be confronted, dealt with, and resolved. Contention, strife, and offenses must be dealt with

in the team. If they are not, the smoldering resentment will spread discontentment through the whole team.

11. *Mutual Encouragement.* Every leader, every member of a ministry team, and every believer needs encouragement from the saints.

> *And Joshua spake unto the priests, saying, Take up the ark of the covenant, and pass over before the people. And they took up the ark of the covenant, and went before the people. And the Lord said unto Joshua, This day will I begin to magnify thee in the sight of all Israel, that they may know that, as I was with Moses, so I will be with thee* (Joshua 3:6-7).

The Lord Himself encouraged Joshua, and we must follow His lead. By encouraging one another, team members will inspire, strengthen, and motivate others to be team players and become fruitful. When morale is low, we should encourage and speak life to uplift one another.

12. *Job Description.* Every team member should ask God for a clearly defined "job description" of his calling and personal ministry. The productivity and achievement of the goals of the team are more easily achieved when every member has a clear picture of his divinely assigned role and task as an individual member of a team.

13. *Communication.* As in any organization, leadership in the church and in the ministry team must positively communicate the vision, aims, and objectives of the church body or movement. Communication is simply the art of clearly sending and receiving messages. Each member of the Body and of the team are expected to hone his communication skills as well.

14. *Leadership*. The ability to lead others into a common vision, goal, or objective is an absolute necessity in the Body of Christ. True leaders must also exhibit the ability to see the needs of people and to equip, train, and develop the gifts in God's people as His resources for the accomplishment of His desires. The leader serves the team members by consistently pointing them to the direction, objectives, goals, and destination of the team.

15. *Servanthood*. By the command and supreme example of Jesus Christ, those who would be great, those who would lead the flock of God, must be the *servant of all*. This is the only attitude and methodology of leadership that is acceptable to God. Yet this is only possible if we know who we are, who has sent us, and why we are sent (see Matt. 20:25-27).

Five Types of Leadership

There are five basic types of leadership and governmental structure common in the world and in the Church. The Church has embraced all but two of them in recent years.

1. *Autocracy*. This form of government features one person who possesses unlimited power and authority while, in theory, answering to no one. The foolish King Rehoboam epitomized this kind of domineering ruler and government (see 1 Kings 12:1-11).

2. *Bureaucracy*. The Pharisees perfectly represent the ultimate hierarchy of authority. This system of leadership is marked by a near-worship of the methodology rather than a concern for ruling wisely or according to a true standard of right and wrong.

3. *Democracy*. This is commonly called "government by the people" and the "rule of the majority." In church circles, it is called congregationalism. Although it sounds good, the

"majority" can be a cruel task master and rarely places truth and right over self and self-serving "majority rule." Its only chance of working is totally dependent on the wisdom, character, and self-restraint of the "majority."

4. *Theocracy.* This term defines the government of a state by immediate divine guidance. In this system, the rule of God is administered through delegated men and women whom He places in the church to represent Him. It only works as long as the people are confident that God actually speaks to men, and secondly, that God speaks to the leaders over them. This was God's chosen governmental method for Israel until her elders formed a committee and "voted" to reject theocracy in favor of the autocracy of a king (see 1 Sam. 8:4-7).

5. *Servant leaders.* The New Testament is filled with examples of servant leaders in action. The greatest servant of all was Jesus, who demonstrated the importance of servanthood in leadership by washing His disciples' feet and commanding them to do the same (see Matt. 20:25-27).[3]

Wise leaders, especially those serving in a ministry team, understand the "four faces of leadership" revealed in Ezekiel 1:10 and fulfilled in Jesus Christ. They also know how to apply each one of them in season:

1. *Face of a man*—Like the Son of man, we must be able to feel the infirmities of others, understand their hurts and needs, and relate to them while sharing their burdens.

2. *Face of a lion*—In times of trouble and times of spiritual warfare, we must know when and how to roar like the Lion of Judah with the authority and awesome power of God that dwells within us.

3. *Face of an ox*—Ministry team members must know what it means to take up the yoke of Jesus and put their shoulder

to the yoke. Hard work and dedication in the face of impossible odds must be engrained in our character.

4. *Face of an eagle*—When the storm clouds approach, we must be able to ascend above the winds, the lightning, and the thunder into the very rest of God. Then we must be able to hear God's voice clearly and to discern and see into the things of God with accuracy.

Structure

One of the most fundamental of all apostolic functions is to establish *structure* or order in the local church. Paul and his disciples were very interested in proper order in the churches:

> *For this reason I left you in Crete, that you should set in order the things that are lacking, and appoint elders in every city as I commanded you* (Titus 1:5 NKJV).

> *For though I am absent in the flesh, yet I am with you in spirit, rejoicing to see your good order and the steadfastness of your faith in Christ* (Colossians 2:5 NKJV).

One of Titus' commissions was to restore what had fallen into disorder. The same is true of apostles and apostolic people today. Historically, the Church gradually began to drift away from the patterns of the early churches. They did not see the need for all the gifts to operate in local churches, so the church was governed by popes, priests, and cardinals. Martin Luther and the Reformation brought governmental structure and order to the Body of Christ.

Areas of Government, Structure, and Order

In the broadest sense, there are seven interrelated areas of the Church that God intended to work together in one great leadership team.

1. There are the fivefold ministry or equipping gifts described by Paul in Ephesians 4. These ministries are called to work together as a team to equip and train the saints for the work of the ministry. There is a genuine need for *all* these ministries in the life of the local church:

   And He Himself gave some to be apostles, some prophets, some evangelists, and some pastors and teachers (Ephesians 4:11 NKJV).

   The *pastor* supplies the vital need for love, care, and affection. The pastor is married to the local church for better or for worse and is an undershepherd standing in place for the Great Shepherd.

   The *teacher* is primarily concerned with the Word of God. If a man is called a pastor but is a teacher, he will always tend to see a church full of people *in need of the Word*. Teachers excel at feeding, but they do not necessarily excel at leading.

   The *evangelist* is after one thing: souls. Even if he is called a pastor, his real motivation as an evangelist is to see the lost saved—even to the point of inadvertently neglecting the needs of the saints.

   Prophets are motivated by revelation and a word from the Lord for the saints. He ministers by revelation, flows in the gifts, and activates the saints in their call. A prophet is also God's communicative channel.

   Apostles are motivated by birthing movements, equipping the saints, raising up sons, training men of ministry, ordaining elders, strengthening churches, and starting new churches.

2. In the thinking of many, a *synonym* for the fivefold ministry gifts are the *elders* or *prebyteros* who rule over the local churches where they are ordained. Paul said, "Let the elders that rule well be counted worthy of double honor, especially they who labour in the word and doctrine" (1 Tim. 5:17). Peter wrote, "Shepherd the flock of God which is among you, serving as overseers, not by compulsion but willingly, not for dishonest gain but eagerly" (1 Pet. 5:2 NKJV).

   In the Book of Acts, Paul the apostle wrote to the elders in his final days before his imprisonment and trial in Jerusalem, "Therefore take heed to yourselves and to all the flock, among which the Holy Spirit has made you overseers, to shepherd the church of God which He purchased with His own blood" (Acts 20:28 NKJV). The responsibility of the elder is to rule, instruct and shepherd. Peter adds that they are to be examples to the flock; they are patterns for others to follow (see 1 Pet. 2-3,5).

3. The elders instituted the office of the deacon in the church at Jerusalem. Paul told Timothy, "Let deacons be the husbands of one wife, ruling their children and their houses well. For those who have served well as deacons obtain for themselves a good standing and great boldness in the faith which is in Christ Jesus" (1 Tim. 3:12-13 NKJV).

4. There are delegated areas of service regarding the day-to-day governing of the church and its many departments or specialized ministry areas.

5. God has given the Church certain skillful and anointed musicians with the anointing of psalmists. Closely linked with this area of ministry are the spontaneous creative arts incorporated in our churches. However, this didn't originate

in the modern era, nor in the late part of the Old Testament. It began when King David the psalmist placed the singer and musicians in place before the Lord to offer up *worship.*

6. We have the "priesthood of all believers" operating side by side with everything else. The result is incredible when we pay the price in prayer to hear God's voice both individually and corporately. Historically the Church did not believe in the priesthood of all believers, but the Scriptures plainly prove that it is so (see 1 Pet. 2:9; Rev. 1:6).

7. There is a divine purpose behind everything God has done since the garden of Eden to this day. That purpose is spelled out in detail in the very first Book of the Bible— God's highest creation is still charged with the work of tending His garden and raising up His most prized creation (mankind). The "work principle" God set in motion in Genesis is still in full operation today, and it has four mandatory elements we must observe as apostolic people today:

   • We must follow God's six-to-one *work ethic,* in which we diligently work in His garden (the world) for six days and rest on the seventh. God created us to work (not relax) most of our days, yet He also commanded us to rest completely for one day as He did. (I have had to learn the principle of rest, or sabbath, through some hard lessons.) (See John 5:17; Genesis 1:4,31.)

   • *Productivity* is to be a hallmark of the Christian life. Fruitfulness was one of the most predominant subjects in Jesus' earthly ministry because it was *important to the Father* (see John 15:2-5).

- *Excellence* is the standard of God, while men prefer the easier standard of "average." In the Book of Genesis, God made two kinds of pronouncements over His work: "good" and "very good" (see Gen. 1:31). The Bible uses the standard of excellence to describe Daniel (Dan. 5:12) and the wise man of understanding in the Book of Proverbs (Prov. 17:27).

- *Time management* is crucial to God's people because we still live within the temporal boundaries of time and space (we still have a birth date and most likely a date of death). God commands us to "redeem the time" as we present the Kingdom to the lost (Col. 4:5; see also Eph. 5:16). Our greatest danger is that of procrastination, which is to intentionally put off or delay doing something that should be done without delay.

When all of these elements blend together in harmonious worship, service, and love, we have a fully functioning Church. The end of the story is really its beginning. God is restoring the office of the *apostle* in order to raise up an *apostolic people*. He is raising up an *apostolic people* to do an *apostolic work* in the earth as He launches worldwide revival and triggers an unprecedented harvest of souls by His Spirit.

As we move closer and closer to His appearing, it is crucial for the Church to be cleansed, purified, raised up, and fired up for the *work of the ministry* and the edifying of itself in love. The apostle is to play a crucial leadership and organizational role in God's plans for the days ahead. It is imperative that we learn how to receive every equipping gift God has given the Church.

If you are called to one of these offices—particularly the office of the apostle—then you must be trained and equipped for the work by those who have gone before you in concert with the work of the Holy Spirit. Above all, each of us must be willing to take up our cross daily and follow after Jesus, the chief apostle and pioneer of our faith, no matter what the cost. Our testimony each day must begin and end with the litany of the servant leader:

I am not my own. For I have been bought with a price: therefore I will glorify God in my body; and in my spirit, which are God's (1 Corinthians 6:19-20, personalized adaptation).

Endnotes

1. NOTE: It is important for leaders to understand that by their very nature, transitions have the possibility of conflict. A wise leader is one who never makes transitions without *first* teaching, evaluating, and knowing where the people stand on the key issues. You should count the costs before you embark on a path of major transition. Be ready to face conflict with various individuals because change always has the possibility of conflict; human beings feel more secure with the known. The unknown always represents risk. Don't allow yourself to be derailed at this point in the transition. Instead, work to gradually introduce new mentalities and philosophies of ministry over a period of time that will bring growth in the saints. Transitions should be gradual. Zeal without wisdom or proper knowledge can easily destroy a movement or local church. I recommend that you seek counsel from others who have made such transitions. In the multitude of counselors, there is wisdom (see Prov. 11:14). Learn from the mistakes and strengths of others so you will be in a better position to avoid their mistakes of the past.

2. See also Numbers 12:2 and the rebellion of Aaron and Miriam.
3. See also Philippians 2:5-8; John 13:3-5.

Bibliography

Blomgren, David K. *Prophetic Gatherings in the Church.* Portland, Oregon: Bible Temple Publishing, 1979.

Cannistraci, David. *The Gift of Apostle.* Ventura, California: Regal Books, 1996.

Conner, Kevin J. *The Foundations of Christian Doctrine.* Bible Temple Publishing, 1989.

_____. and K. Patrick Conner. *Church in the New Testament.* Bible Temple Publishing, 1998.

Damazio, Frank. *The Vanguard Leader.* Portland, Oregon: Bible Temple, 1994.

Eckhardt, John. *The Ministry Anointing of the Apostle.* Chicago, Illinois: Crusaders Publications, 1993.

Genenius, H.F.W. *Hebrew-Chaldee Lexicon to the Old Testament.* Grand Rapids, Michigan: Baker Book House, 1980.

Gordan, Bob and David Fardouly. *Master Builders.* Kent, England: Sovereign World, 1990.

Hamon, Bill. *Prophets and the Prophetic Movement.* Shippensburg, Pennsylvania: Destiny Image, 1990.

Iverson, Dick. Grant, Ray. *Team Ministry.* Portland, Oregon: Bible Temple Publishing, 1984.

Kittel, Gerhard. *Theological Dictionary of the New Testament.* Grand Rapids, Michigan: WM.B. Eerdmans Publishing, 1964.

Louton, Ed. *Missions and the Kingdom.* White River, South Africa: Southern Africa Seminars, 1989.

Nee, Watchman. *The Church and the Work 2.* New York: Christian Fellowship Publishers, 1982.

Richards, Lawrence O. *Expository Dictionary of Bible Words.* Grand Rapids, Michigan: Zondervan Publishers, 1991.

Sapp, Roger. *The Last Apostles on Earth.* Shippensburg, Pennsylvania: Companion Press, 1995.

Tenney, Merrill C., ed. *The Zondervan Pictoral Encyclopedia of the Bible.* Grand Rapids, Michigan: Zondervan Publishing House, 1975.

Wagner, Peter C. *Lighting the World.* Ventura, California: Regal Books, 1995.

Zodhiates, Spiros; *The Complete Word Study Dictionary New Testament.* Chattanooga, Tennessee: AMG Publishers, 1992.

_____. *The Complete Word Study New Testament.* AMG International, 1992.

_____. *Conquering the Fear of Death.* Chattanooga, Tennessee: AMG Publishers, 1970.

Also by Robert Munien:

Understanding the Seasons of God

Write or call to order copies:

In the United States:

Sent Forth Ministries Int'l. Inc.
826 Tallow Hill Road
Chambersburg, PA 17201

Phone: 717-264-4438
FAX: 717-597-1160
Email: sentfrth@epix.net

In South Africa:

Robert Munien
P.O. Box 60054
Phoenix 4068
Kwa-Zulu Natal
Republic of South Africa

Phone: 27-31-5023655
FAX: 27-31-5023656
Email: Munien@icon.co.za